SOCIAL
BUTTERFLIES

SOCIAL
BUTTERFLIES

Reclaiming the Positive Power of Social Networks

Michael Sanders and Susannah Hume

Michael O'Mara Books Limited

First published in Great Britain in 2019
by Michael O'Mara Books Limited
9 Lion Yard
Tremadoc Road
London SW4 7NQ

A CIP catalogue record for this book is available from the British Library.

Papers used by Michael O'Mara Books Limited are natural,
recyclable products made from wood grown in sustainable forests.
The manufacturing processes conform to the environmental
regulations of the country of origin.

ISBN: 978-1-78243-957-8 in hardback print format
ISBN: 978-1-78929-117-9 in trade paperback print format
ISBN: 978-1-78243-978-3 in ebook format

1 2 3 4 5 6 7 8 9 10

www.mombooks.com

Designed and typeset by Ed Pickford

Printed and bound by CPI Group (UK) Ltd, Croydon, CR0 4YY

Contents

Introduction

We are all social animals. Our social instincts and propensity to form and sustain groups with shared loyalties, motives and culture are in many ways *the* story of humanity. Without the social part of ourselves there could be no societies. Without the ability to work together we couldn't develop organized and structured agriculture. Without agriculture we couldn't have moved into towns; and without the capacity to get along and forge shared identities we couldn't have survived for long in those towns, let alone in the complex, interconnected communities and structures we now inhabit.

In the twenty-first century, more than ever before, we behave as social butterflies. We're able to move between social categories and groups at will, and we now have unprecedented and numerous means to communicate with each other. But we're also butterflies in another way. Chaos theory suggests that the changing of something very small – the flap of a butterfly's wings – can have a disproportionate influence on the world. As social butterflies, we influence others in ways that we don't always realize and we, in turn, are unwittingly influenced by others. These influences are, at least in part, responsible for many of the wonderful things in the world: culture, sport, the formation and cementing of friendships, and our charitable behaviours.

But our instinct to get along with others can also lead us in less positive directions. In September 2007, in one of the earliest manifestations of what would become the 2007–8 Global Financial Crisis, the British bank Northern Rock found itself short of money to pay its debts. When news of this became public, there was concern among the bank's customers about the security of their deposits. Of course, with the Bank of England providing a financial backstop, the overwhelming majority of deposits were safe; yet some customers withdrew their funds regardless, presumably having decided that the cash would be safer in their own hands.

This may have begun as a slow drip of customers withdrawing their money, but it soon became a torrent; as it gained attention in the press, more customers saw what was happening and decided to follow suit. No one wanted to be the last one standing when the music stopped. So began the first 'run' on a bank in the UK for 150 years.

By this point, with trust in the bank low and a norm established of extracting cash, no amount of reassurance from the bank could settle the public panic. On 22 February 2008, the British government announced that it would nationalize Northern Rock. Six months later, when the US investment bank Lehman Brothers collapsed and wasn't bailed out, the global financial crisis exploded in earnest.

Even as the crisis unfolded, many experts and academics maintained that there wouldn't – *couldn't* – be a run on a bank in the developed Western world. This was not simply a matter of the law, or of history. This was a belief, hardbaked into conventional economic thought, that people would behave rationally: that they would not engage in behaviour that ran counter to their own interests. The loss of trust in the bank, despite the law, showed that trust was a matter of feelings and not just of facts. Traditional economic theories couldn't explain why a few malcontents withdrawing their cash could so rapidly become tens of thousands of people doing the same – you shouldn't join someone you see behaving irrationally, after all.

Along with the emergence of the subprime mortgage bubble, and the seeming powerlessness of governments to stop the crisis once it had begun, failure of economic thought to come to grips with the behaviour unfolding led to the beginning of a more wholesale rejection of economics. Instead, people began to turn towards a fairly small subsection of the discipline – *behavioural economics* – that sought, through the marriage of economics and psychology, to explain and predict human behaviour better than either discipline could by itself.

Although the field had already caught on to a great extent in academia – Daniel Kahneman and Amos Tversky published the foundational paper, 'Prospect theory',[1] in 1979, and Kahneman had won the economics Nobel Prize in 2002[2] – it had yet to grip either the popular consciousness or policymakers. The financial crisis, as well as the publication of Richard Thaler and Cass Sunstein's book *Nudge* in 2008,[3] changed all of that. If the crisis showed that policymakers couldn't rely on the models of traditional economists, which had failed to predict the subprime mortgage problem *and* consumers' reactions to it, *Nudge* gave both an alternative approach to understanding behaviour and, more importantly, suggestions about how to do things better next time. Determined to put these lessons to work, Sunstein joined the Obama administration to run the office of information and regulatory affairs – one of the less well known, but most influential parts of the US government.

Over the last few years, governments around the world have sought out the guidance of Thaler and Sunstein – and their followers – and so-called Nudge Units have sprung up in droves.

The first of these was the British government's Behavioural Insights Team, or BIT, where we both worked – Susannah for the last five years, and Michael for the last seven. BIT's remit is to apply the new thinking coming out of behavioural economics and related fields to some of the complex problems faced by the UK government. In practice this often comes down to paying attention to how people actually approach decisions – whether to withdraw all their money from their bank, for example, or whether to go to university – rather than how we think they should approach decisions, or how they say they approach them.

This may seem obvious, but for many years this way of thinking was not common in the corridors of power: economists, and their theories of rational, selfish individuals, reigned supreme. When BIT first formed in 2010, it was groundbreaking for two reasons. First, it brought a more realistic model of human behaviour, based on psychological insights about how we really think, into the corridors of power. Second, it relied much less on theory, and much more on data, than a lot of what had gone before it – bringing randomized experiments, like those used in medicine, into policymaking in a major way for the first time. This combination of scientific methodology and the use of government power to help people was what first attracted both of us to BIT.

Much of what has followed from the great recession, from *Nudge* and from the behavioural revolution in economics, focuses on our cognitive failures, or behavioural biases – the shortcomings in our brain and the tricks it plays on us that lead us to behave as we do. There has been less focus, so far, on the complex tangle of social threads in which we are all entwined. Our aim with this book is to turn our gaze on this tangle, to try to understand its different components and how they can be influenced. At a basic level, *social influence* refers to the ways in which our emotions, judgements and actions are influenced by those around us, our *social environment*, which comprises what we observe others doing, what cues we get from them about what we should do and what information is flowing through our network (the way that we learn about a new restaurant from friends, for example). Generally, this is driven by instinct, which, at a deep level, drives us to seek safety with others. Some social groups, such as our friends, family and colleagues – our network – can be small and interactive, while others are more symbolic and linked to our gender, ethnicity, beliefs, political affiliations and so on.

Although this can seem commonsensical, perhaps even obvious, the effects of our social instincts are often much larger than we imagine. Like that butterfly flapping its wings half a world away and causing a tsunami, a small ripple in the fabric of our social environment can have big effects on not only our own decisions, but also the decisions of those we influence in turn: our friends, family and networks. When we compare ourselves to our neighbours, or try to impress them, or make choices that follow the pack, either consciously or unconsciously, we are in the grip of these forces.

The behavioural economics revolution brought with it the beginning of an awareness of the effects of ripples through social networks, and these effects have been amplified by another revolution – less sudden, subtler but ultimately, we suspect, more impactful – in studying social influence. If people's social instincts were powerful enough to help start a recession, then they've become if anything *more* powerful over the intervening decade. The rise of social media has sent our social instincts into overdrive. Facebook lets us compare ourselves to thousands of our friends in a single day, while on Instagram we can spend hours contemplating not just what to wear in our holiday snaps to maximize peer envy but also which hashtags will reach and affect the most people.

As our decision-making is increasingly influenced by our social instincts and social networks, everyone from tech firms to aspiring politicians has begun trying to work out how to use them for their own purposes. Social media platforms have become more powerful, and our actual relationships with the people we're 'connected' with on them become more tenuous. As a consequence, spreading deception across our networks and watching it take hold has become easier – as has destroying trust on a massive scale. Companies like Cambridge Analytica stand accused of industrial levels of manipulation, using advanced statistical techniques married to psychological insight. They are alleged to have achieved this by accessing data on 50 million Facebook users – everything they liked, who their friends were and how they responded to various surveys. Using this data, they built up a profile of each person and put them into categories based on algorithms developed to assess what users were most likely to be influenced by. People could then be sent different (and very often fake) news stories according to these categorizations – with the aim of getting them to buy certain products, or vote in a particular way. The company's activities on Facebook have been linked to both the EU referendum in the UK and the 2016 presidential election in the US – in both cases, they used Facebook's data and infrastructure to support the side that ended up winning.

As human beings, we have found ourselves in a world that we're not well-equipped evolutionarily to navigate. Our social instincts, which allowed us to seek safety in groups, and to co-ordinate activities that protected these groups, have not prepared us well for a globalized, interdependent world, where people seeking to manipulate us can follow us into our homes, our relationships and our electronic devices.

However, although this is undoubtedly true, we should be wary of concentrating on the negatives. It is too easy to forget the power of our social groups to give us safety, esteem and wellbeing, and the potent and wonderful ways in which people can reach out across their networks – and across the world – to help others. This is the journey we hope this book travels on: from where we are, to where we could be if we sought to understand the beauty and strength of the social – and how it can help us make the world a better place.

To do this we must start by exploring the world as it is now, to understand how our sense of who we are and how we fit into our social world has formed – and has been manipulated. The common phrase 'us and them' goes to a deeply rooted aspect of human psychology, which is that we are wired to see people as part of either an 'us' (a social group to which we also belong), or as a 'them' (not like us, and not part of our group) – and to prefer those we consider 'us' over those we consider 'them'.

In Part 1 of the book, we introduce the dynamics of intergroup interactions – on one hand, the interactions between people who see each other as belonging to different social groups ('them'); and on the other, interactions between people who see each other as part of the same 'us'. We explore how easily people come to identify with an 'us', how quickly we start to prefer those in the group and dislike and distrust those outside it, and how this leads to stereotyping and discrimination. We also go inside the group and look at how a strong sense of group membership – and a fear of being kicked out – leads to conformity, policing the behaviour of others and undertaking risky or self-defeating activities in order to stay close to the group. And we look at this in the context of social media: how it has changed the terms of our interactions with others within and beyond our groups; and how companies are now trying to turn this to their own ends, to make money or swing elections.

The last fifteen years provide material for a dozen books on the topic of social influence and its ills. But when it comes to the power of social influence this is just a part of the story, an albeit dramatic and often far-reaching one. The fact is that our social instincts are not a weakness to be overcome in order to help us meet our potential, but are instead an integral part of who we are and of our success as a species. We can't stop being social any more than we can stop breathing. So, the question is: how do we maximize the good – and minimize the bad – that arises from our social instincts?

This question is the focus of the second two parts of the book. In Part 2, we take a leaf out of Thaler and Sunstein's *Nudge* and introduce *social choice architecture* – the ways in which our environments shape our behaviour, with either positive or negative effects. Thaler and Sunstein encouraged governments to take up their role as choice architects, and to deploy nudges alongside traditional government tools of taxation, legislation and information. Much of nudging consists of designing physical environments – such as whether fruits or sweets are closest to the cash register in a cafeteria, or how communications, information and even forms are structured. These physical structures can subtly influence our behaviour.

Likewise, we are highly influenced by our social environment, so social choice architecture considers how designing the social environment can enable us to mobilize social influence for good. In doing this, we need to explore in more detail the functioning of social groups, and how people come to see themselves as members of particular groups, which can act as the boundaries of effective social nudging. As well as examining ways to reduce some of the negatives, including negative stereotyping and discrimination, we explore the importance of what psychologists call social distance; that is, how socially 'close' or 'distant' we perceive someone else to be, because of our interpersonal relationships or shared social identities.

We also need to look at how information travels through networks. Norms are our understanding of what the dominant behaviour is in our group, but we can often have inaccurate perceptions of the prevailing norms. We can create positive behaviour change by providing correct information about positive norms or reducing information about negative norms – for instance, we can reduce energy consumption by making high consumers aware they are above the average, but telling people that there is low uptake of energy-saving devices is likely to backfire. Importantly, we look too at how we can improve the distribution of this positive information, and why some information travels better than others.

Understanding these social dynamics helps us design the context around important decisions to encourage people to make good choices for themselves and those around them. But as even diehard fans would attest, nudges can go only so far. Beyond that, we need to look at the overall shape of the social groups people belong to, and the resources they have at their disposal as a result of those groups in terms of advice, support (financial and otherwise) and access to opportunities – in other words, their *social capital*. The limitations of nudges here are obvious. If people's connections to their groups are weak, social nudges aren't going to help much. If the groups have bad norms – either because most people don't engage in positive behaviours, or because the group doesn't support its members in particular ways – the benefits of social nudges will be difficult to realize. Finally, if our social groups connect us only to people in the same situation as us, those networks will not be able to lift our sights to new horizons, or pull us into a different and better life.

In the final part of this book we take a look at three types of intervention to influence the social capital at people's disposal. We will look at how we can mobilize people's existing networks to more effectively support them to achieve difficult but valuable goals. We'll also look at ways to help people build social bridges – positive relationships with people in new groups that can both ease transitions and allow the myths that come with social distance to be overcome. Lastly, we look at two things that happen when things go right in the social world: belongingness and trust. Belongingness is the feeling of being somewhere we fit – where we are wanted and accepted. It is one of the most powerful (and necessary) feelings for our wellbeing, and we get it from strong, well-functioning social groups. Social trust is the feeling that most people around us can be trusted, which is a benefit of strong social capital.

Our aim with this book is to sketch out a roadmap to a society where there is more belonging, more trust and – we hope – less discrimination and conformity. We believe that our social selves are, overall, a force for good in the world, leading to many of the best facets of our society – something we may take for granted. We want to show that, although our social instincts can be hijacked by nefarious forces, the world as we know it would crumble without them.

More importantly, we hope you'll understand how small changes to our environment can make a big difference in whether those social instincts lead us down a path for good or for ill. The insights that we've gathered from our own research and experience, and the innovators and academics around the world, are widely applicable to anywhere our social selves can either give us a boost or trip us up – from the way we lead our personal lives to the way we work and study to the way we manage or lead organizations. But before we're able to reclaim the positive power of our social networks, we need first to understand what – and who – it is that we're reclaiming them from, and how these have earned an often deserved reputation for leading us astray.

PART 1

The State of
Social Influence

1

Them

'Collective fear stimulates herd instinct, and tends to produce ferocity toward those who are not regarded as members of the herd.'

Bertrand Russell

JOHN YOSSARIAN, THE main character of the Second World War novel *Catch-22*, is obsessed with the fact that the Germans are trying to kill him. It's nothing personal, he's told; it's because he's American and America is at war with Germany. But Yossarian doesn't buy this argument: 'And what difference does that make?' he asks. As far as he's concerned, someone trying to kill him is pretty personal regardless of whether or not they know it's him they're trying to kill.

During our lifetime we encounter thousands of people: our family and friends, work colleagues, strangers on the street, sales staff in stores, celebrities on TV and people on the news. Some – such as our family, friends and work colleagues – we interact with personally. But others we interact with more as members of a group. For instance, generally, when a man holds a door open for a woman he doesn't know, it's not because of who she is as a person; it's because of her gender, and a norm he (and possibly she) subscribes to. When a pedestrian steps on to the cycleway causing a cyclist to brake sharply to avoid them and then think, 'Pedestrians are idiots,' the cyclist is not thinking about that person, who might usually be very careful on cycleways but had been distracted because of something that happened earlier that day. Instead, the cyclist is interacting with a member of a group (pedestrians) who are in his view generally idiots.

On a day-to-day level, we can think of the purely personal as being a conversation between friends about what they did at the weekend, while a purely *intergroup* example – one between members of two different and rival groups – might be the interaction between two fans supporting opposing teams at a football match. In the first case, the interaction is focused on the two people involved, while the second isn't really about the individuals; it's about the social identities associated with their teams.

Yossarian's refusal to distinguish between Germans trying to kill *all* Americans and Germans trying to kill him personally is understandable, but it goes against the grain of how we see the world. We may not like the idea of people trying to harm other people, but we instinctively feel that there's a difference between conflict that's 'personal' and conflict that's about group objectives, beliefs or interests.

This categorization is generally a useful habit: it simplifies a complex world and can help us avoid danger by causing us to avoid people fitting into the social group of, for example, 'man lurking in dark alleyway'. And finding a common group can help mobilize people to support and protect each other. Our sense of who we are and what we believe – our identity – is partly formed by the social groups to which we belong.

But, in recent years, identity and particularly identity politics has come to mean something altogether less positive – a means by which we can be driven apart rather than brought together. If we're going to move past the darkness and work out how to make a positive impact, it's essential that we understand the dark side of our instinct to seek our social groups, and how it can polarize people and lead them to commit terrible acts.

The study of conflict between groups, as with much modern scholarship on social influence, grew out of one of the darkest periods of the twentieth century. Henri Tajfel, a Polish Jew, served in the French Army in the Second World War and survived a series of prisoner-of-war camps, returning home to find his entire family had fallen victim to the Nazis.[4] When captured, Tajfel concealed his Polish heritage from his German guards – because while a French Jew might survive as a POW, a Polish Jew certainly wouldn't. This experience of living under a different identity, and knowing that that group membership mattered more to his survival than anything else, drove Tajfel's intellectual interest in social identity and intergroup conflict.

What he wanted to understand was how people could reach the point of hating and distrusting others they had never met, and had no personal grudge against, enough to condone harm being done to them – or even to inflict it themselves. Tajfel's research was driven by his belief that no matter how good his relationship with the German guards was on an interpersonal level, if they had known he was a Polish Jew, he would have been killed. Had his full identity – as both Jewish and Polish – been discovered, it would have been these categories that determined how the guards treated him. His other characteristics, and the guards' experiences of him, would have been irrelevant to them.[5] In the blink of an eye, the person they liked could become a member of a hated group.

We go through life carrying with us a set of social groups to which we belong, a set of beliefs (or stereotypes) about the social groups to which others belong, and an innate tendency to want the groups to which we belong to be better than rival groups. Believing that our group is better, or just wanting them to do better, can lead us to favour our group over others when we get the chance – in short, to discriminate against other groups. This affects the way in which we decide who gets to join our groups, and even such seemingly unrelated decisions as our willingness to buy and sell goods and for what price.

In recent years, it has become increasingly clear that this isn't always overt, out-and-out discrimination, which is comparatively easy to identify and (where the will exists) penalize. Instead, a lot of discrimination in our daily lives occurs as a result of biases that are subtle; we might not even be aware of them, but they nonetheless change our behaviour towards members of other groups – these are what psychologists call *implicit biases*.

Identifying when discrimination is caused by these implicit biases is hard because there's a lot going on. For example, the legacy of centuries of slavery and decades of policies that segregated people along ethnic lines has left people of African descent in Europe and North America with a range of disadvantages behind which implicit discriminators can hide to justify their actions.

One study highlighted this issue really clearly. CVs were produced that were identical except for one regard: the names of the candidates. Some featured stereotypically African-American names, while stereotypically 'white' names were chosen for others. These CVs were then sent out – nearly 5,000 times – for job applications. CVs with white names got 50 per cent more call-backs than identical CVs with African-American names[6] – a figure

18

that didn't vary much depending on whether the candidates were male or female, or the type of job being applied for.

In everything, from who we hire to who we let stay in our Airbnb apartment, researchers have uncovered subtle discrimination against particular groups, such as women and people of minority ethnic backgrounds.

We are wired to seek out shared social groups with those we encounter. It is also surprisingly easy to sow the seeds of a new shared group identity. In a series of experiments, Tajfel and his collaborators explored just how little it can take for humans to form social groups and start to discriminate against each other. In one experiment, teenaged students were asked whether they preferred the paintings of Kandinsky or Klee, and were then put in groups with other students they were told had chosen the same painter. These experiments, known as the 'minimal group experiments',[7] found that even such a minor thing as a choice between two painters could result in the development of social identities, and be followed by in-group bias and distrust of the other.

Another early study that draws attention to this is the Robbers Cave study.[8] In this experiment, twenty-two boys aged eleven and twelve were taken to a residential camp at the Robbers Cave State Park in Oklahoma, where they spent several weeks. They were divided into two groups and during the first week were encouraged to bond; they gradually developed their own group identities, taking on team names (the 'Rattlers' and the 'Eagles') and hierarchies of their own devising. In many ways, the experiment is a case study in how to create good social ties – in less than a week, the boys were able to form a functioning if juvenile society. The dark side of this bonding came about when two groups were introduced to each other, and immediately an intense rivalry formed. With only gentle encouragement from the researchers leading the experiment, the groups' conflict escalated from name-calling to robbery and theft, and to the burning of the other team's flags.

Even though the children began the camp with what psychologists call low social distance – they were all the same age, male, protestant and lower middle class – within two weeks their new social identities led to conflict immune to the experimenters' initial attempts to overcome it. This shows us how quickly we can form a new social group under the right circumstances – and how strong the bonds within the group can become. When we start a new job, or join a new volleyball team, we come quickly to identify with our teammates.

Organizations (and volleyball-team captains) might work hard to form a team identity, through precisely the kind of activities that the Rattlers and Eagles went through – and they will probably be pretty effective. When building a team, rituals – whether they're weekly stand-up meetings or monthly drinks – and visual markers of group membership, such as mugs or a particular make of laptop, will start to cement shared identities.

These group identities make the team stronger – making people pull together to meet a deadline, finish a product or win a volleyball league – but they also set us up in opposition to other groups. When that happens, the consequences can be a lot more serious than adolescent flag burning, especially when there's a power imbalance at play.

So, we are members of myriad social groups, from the family unit all the way up to groups based on things such as gender, ethnicity and sexuality. Which of these social groups is at the forefront of someone's mind depends on the situation surrounding an interaction, and what people are expecting to see in that situation – often based on incomplete information. At any given time, changing the lines along which a debate is happening – from being about a group that encompasses everyone involved (for instance, Briton) to identities that divide (Brexiteer and Remainer) – can create the conditions for intergroup conflict that can quickly become toxic and take decades, or centuries, to repair.

This splitting and re-forming is a usual part of political cycles. During an election, people split along party lines, but after the election is over they need to come back together as a nation. For a long time, it was expected that the loser of a political contest would throw his (or, occasionally, her) weight into the task of reasserting the shared national identity that united former political opponents. One of the most famous examples of this is the 1952 concession speech of Adlai Stevenson, who lost the presidential election to Dwight D. Eisenhower: 'That which unites us as American citizens is far greater than that which divides us as political parties [...] We vote as many. But we pray as one.'

Since the early 2000s another trend in political campaigning has been developing, which tries to exploit the fault lines within social groups to win elections. This 'dog-whistle' politics drives groups apart by focusing attention on the issues that divide them.

This strategy will be familiar to Australian readers from the 2001 Federal Election. Supporters of the Australian Labor Party fell broadly into two groups: the 'Latte-sipping Lefties', inner-city professional Labor voters; and the 'Aussie Battlers', the traditional working-class base of the party. These groups had coexisted within the party since the 1970s because the issues they agreed on

– workers' rights, social welfare and so on – were more important than their differences. Their shared partisan identity was at the forefront. But one thing they disagreed on was border protection. On the one hand, Latte-sipping Lefties favoured open borders and high migration and they welcomed asylum seekers, particularly those coming by boat from Indonesia. On the other hand, Aussie Battlers favoured a tougher stance, particularly towards the so-called 'boat people'.

In the run-up to the election, a couple of incidents occurred where boats containing asylum seekers were intercepted and either prevented from entering Australian waters or turned around. The Conservative Coalition government brought these cases to the forefront of people's minds, emphasizing national sovereignty ('We decide who comes to this country, and the circumstances in which they come'), fairness (these asylum seekers were 'queue jumpers', trying to circumvent the formal asylum resettlement process), and family values (the government encouraged reports that some asylum seekers had thrown their children overboard to force the nearby Australian patrol ship to intervene). Latte-sipping Lefties and Aussie Battlers disagreed vehemently on these issues, with the Labor Party itself trying to avoid alienating either group. By focusing on asylum seekers as a key election issue, the Coalition was able to take the shared partisan group that had united the Latte-sipping Lefties and the Aussie Battlers and split it into two – and in doing so brought enough of the Battlers over to its side to win the election.

The tactic is effective – widening fault lines in society and picking on particular groups to separate them from their traditional allies wins elections. The problem is, those rifts don't miraculously close themselves once election night is over. Instead the losing side is left bruised and unable, or unwilling, to help bring people back together again. Politicians who seek wedge issues drive groups further and further apart, and invest less in healing the divisions in between elections. Giving some evidence of this, election surveys have increasingly found that the American electorate is polarized, and that 'Democrat' and 'Republican' constitute distinct social groups complete with positive self-perceptions and negative stereotypes about the other side – and this partisan stereotyping has increased by more than 50 per cent since the time of Eisenhower and Stevenson[9].

Another, more recent, example is the 2016 American presidential election. The white social group is one of the most powerful – and ignored – identities in politics, but off the back of Donald Trump's explicit targeting of this group during his presidential campaign (during which the dog whistle sometimes became a megaphone), it's been interesting to look at how drawing attention to white identity influences voting preferences. One study found that reminding white subjects that non-white people will outnumber whites in the US by 2042 caused them to report more support for Trump and less support for pro-immigration policies – unsurprisingly, this effect occurred particularly among those who reported strong white ethnic identity.[10]

The gradual rise of wedge politics, and the strengthening of divergent identities, paints Donald Trump's election in a different light. Instead of a stand-out event, in which control of first the Republican party and then the whole country was seized by a 'hostile takeover', Trumpism is in fact the culmination of a more gradual process of partisan polarization.

A large segment of the American voter base identify as white, Christian and working class – social groups that might previously have suggested conflicting partisan affiliations. So, for example, being white suggested a loose affiliation with the Republican party, but being working class more commonly led people towards the trade union movement and made them more likely to vote for the Democrats. Now, however, these different groups – white, working class and Christian – are increasingly aligned with the Republicans. The less conflict there is between the different types of groups we place ourselves in, the more our affiliation is cemented, making us favour other members of our own group and tolerate other groups even less.[11]

Donald Trump's slogan, 'Make America Great Again' (or #MAGA) has been generally recognized to have been a wedge to separate racially conservative white voters from the larger bloc of Democrat-leaning lower-income voters and draw them across to his side[12] by calling back to a mythical bygone America where things were fair and safe – and, incidentally, very white. Trump spoke directly to these voters; and he promised them that if *he* won, America would win and they would win.

In her concession speech, Hillary Clinton said, 'We have seen that our nation is more deeply divided than we thought. But I still believe in America, and I always will. And if you do, then we must accept this result and then look to the future. Donald Trump is going to be our president. We owe him an open mind and the chance to lead. Our constitutional democracy enshrines the peaceful transfer of power.' A recognition of partisan division that is a far cry from Stevenson's 'That which unites us …'

The 2016 presidential election will undoubtedly keep political scientists occupied for decades, but from a social influence perspective it is a striking marker on the road towards what may be a breakdown of the two-party system in the US. We saw diverse groups of voters who had historically aligned under the Democrat banner separated from each other as predominantly lower-income white voters were swayed by a right-wing populist who tapped into fears over immigration and jobs – just as supporting Brexit in the UK has brought together the anti-capitalist left with the conservative right. These differences were always there. People within broad social groupings such as political affiliations will always disagree on some things, just like staff within an organization will have a diverse set of identities and interests or people in a volleyball team might have different priorities, outlooks and identities. Societies, organizations and volleyball teams work because the people in them agree that the shared project of the group is more important than the issues individual members perhaps disagree on.

What we have seen in politics over the last decade, particularly in the US and UK, is an unravelling of that agreement. Politicians look to win by 'wedging' their opponents' support base, and there is no collaboration afterwards over bringing the country back together – in fact, we often see the arguments of the election campaign carried forward into the governing period. A company that ran with that level of conflict would quickly fold, and very few people would choose to stay in a volleyball team where the members weren't willing to concentrate on working as a team to try to win the game. A country, however, continues to limp on amid such rising divisions.

But what happens if, instead of looking to break up a group, the whole group is attacked. These are known as *identity threats*, because they represent threats related to a social group with which we may identify or be identified.

Identity threats can evoke the same kind of physiological response that our ancestors experienced when they came across evidence of a predator. It focuses the mind on the threat, narrows the focus and creates a physical stress response that prepares us for our most basic of reactions: fight or flight. The fact that you're here, reading this book, probably means that your ancestors were good at detecting threats and responding this way – that, or they were incredibly lucky.

We can think of identity threats as taking three broad forms: threats to the group; threats to the individual's place within the group; and threats of being categorized into the group. In the case of our pedestrian and cyclist we see an example of the first instance: the hurled abuse might challenge the pedestrian's perception that the group to which they belong is superior to motorists, cyclists, scooter users, rollerbladers and so on.

The second type of identity threat can take the form of challenging our perception of closeness to the ideal of the identity (for instance, one gym-goer to another might say, 'Do you even lift, bro?'), or challenging our ability to do things that are inconsistent with that identity. And the third, categorization threat, refers to the potential of being designated part of a group that we don't identify with (particularly if it's a low-status group). We look at these latter two in more detail in the next chapter.

On 9 September 2016, Hillary Clinton addressed a campaign fundraising event in New York City. To a warm and sympathetic room, she said: 'You could put half of Trump's supporters into what I call the "basket of deplorables". Right? They're racist, sexist, homophobic, xenophobic, Islamophobic – you name it. And unfortunately, there are people like that.' These comments were widely covered and created some backlash.

What's particularly interesting, though, is the reaction of the Deplorables themselves. When we experience an identity threat

there are, broadly, six types of response we can make: attacking and discrediting the attacker;[13] concealing our affiliation to the identity; arguing in favour of the identity; ceasing to relate to the identity; changing our perception of the identity; or reducing how important that identity is to us. Which of these responses we take depends on our circumstances, the strength of our affiliation to the identity and the nature of the threat.

Clinton might have hoped that branding a subset of Trump supporters *deplorable* would cause voting for Trump to be less appealing, but in fact it seems to have had the opposite effect. The so-called deplorables adopted the term for themselves and used it to strengthen their sense of themselves as a collective identity. They changed the meaning of their identity to encompass a group concept of being marginalized by the establishment.

Attacking the source of the threat as a response is perhaps the easiest of the six responses to demonstrate. In 2012, Anita Sarkeesian, a Canadian-American video blogger, posted a crowdfunding campaign to fund a series of videos exploring the ways that women were portrayed in video games. This set off a wave of harassment from male video gamers – from hacking her personal details to death threats and even the development of a flash game where users could punch her face, which got successively more bruised. In this instance, a particular segment of the online community experienced Sarkeesian's action as a threat to the positive distinctiveness of their identity as 'video gamers', since it could be taken to mean that video games were sexist, and they didn't consider themselves – or their games – sexist. They responded by attacking and attempting to discredit Sarkeesian.

This type of response to identity threats from females to identities encompassing masculinity is, unfortunately, not unusual.

One lab experiment found that, among a group of young men, particularly those who identified strongly with masculinity, the level of harassment directed towards women increased when the men experienced a threat to the legitimacy (interacting with a 'feminist' woman) or positive distinctiveness (receiving feedback that women were performing better) of their identity, or their own closeness to being an ideal member of the group (being informed that they were an 'atypical' male).[14]

In *Catch-22*, Yossarian responds to the threat of being shot at by ceasing to identify with the social group of USAF bombardier captain and its associated rules and expectations. Unfortunately, in the middle of the war he can't just reassign, so he spends most of the novel trying to turn his psychological exiting of the group into a physical escape from his post, and away from all the people – both German and American – who are trying to kill him. Henri Tajfel concealed his identity as a Polish Jew in order to survive the POW camp. Centuries before this, the *conversos* in Portugal and Spain survived the same way, by converting to Christianity in public but preserving their Jewish faith in secret. But this kind of concealment has costs: one study found that people who conceal stigmatized identities in the workplace in the hope that this will increase their acceptance can find doing so has the opposite effect,[15] leading to lower wellbeing and workplace performance.

So where does all this leave us? It seems clear that our social selves are at their worst when we're being encouraged to deepen our affiliation to people like us, and to hate, distrust and act against people who don't share our social groups. However, this state of deepening identification with a narrow set of social groups creates challenges from within as well.

2

Us

'Some people did what their neighbours did, so that if any lunatics were at large, one might know and avoid them.'

Middlemarch, George Eliot

I N 2017, MICHAEL interviewed for an academic job. The behavioural economics revolution was in full swing and, although it was cultivating its own rebel-outsider image, this new way of thinking had been fairly widely accepted. It was therefore a bit surprising that half of the hour-long interview was spent with one interviewer insistently and repeatedly asking whether Michael's work in behavioural economics was really economics at all, and whether he even belonged in a department like theirs – the same kind of department in which he had trained as an economist for more than a decade. Needless to say, Michael didn't get the job.

At first glance, Michael's experience has a lot in common with the situations we discussed in the previous chapter – a threat to his identity as an economist, in the form of another economist telling him he had no place in an economics department. But this example is different. In the last chapter we were looking at *inter*group conflict – conflict between groups – but Michael's interview experience is actually *intra*group conflict, occurring between two members of the same group: in this case, economists. And what was being challenged was Michael's place in the group.

We've looked at how members of the same group are disposed to like each other, and seek to agree with each other. But what about when they disagree? What about when two members who identify with the same social group diverge systematically about what it means to be a member of that group?

When we take on membership of a social group and internalize it, we go through a process of (self) stereotyping: we develop a mental image about what it means to be a member of that group, and we then strive to conform to that ideal. This is a social process – individuals sharing a social group will seek to reach agreement about what group membership entails, and how the group provides collective esteem or value to its members. Because this process is social, and the behaviour of others in the group affects the esteem or value we accrue from membership, we would prefer it if everyone in the group acts in a way we'd like, and we'd prefer others not to join if they're going to change the meaning of the group.

This problem often occurs in small, growing companies. As the organization changes – from a start-up to a medium-sized company, for example – the original staff, who are probably closely socially linked to each other and have a strong image of what it means to work for the organization, can start to feel like the organizational identity is getting diluted by newcomers who may not share the same outlook. Likewise, newcomers can feel like they're facing a 'closed shop' that doesn't really welcome their contributions. Moving from a small, interactive social group to something larger, more symbolic and more institutionalized is one of the biggest challenges for small enterprises looking to scale up – it often fails, and can take the organization down with it. How much we'll police the borders of a social group depends on how strongly we identify with it, and how easy it is to 'exit' in favour of another group.

Our level of attachment to a group also changes how acceptable we find other people's violations of the group's expected behaviour. People react to deviant members of a group they are strongly affiliated with; they may perceive either that their own membership might be threatened if the deviant member's behaviour becomes the new 'normal', or that the deviant member's behaviour reduces the esteem or value people derive from the group. We'll probably react more strongly to deviant members in a workplace where we're trying to get promoted than if one of the members of our knitting circle takes up crochet.

So, our sense of belonging to a group, and the value we attach to the group and our place in it, depends on both how other people in the group behave and how similar we ourselves are to the ideal. To try to maintain the group – and our place in it – we can encourage others to conform to the rules of the group as we see them. But what about when things get so bad that someone – either ourselves or another – faces ejection from the group entirely?

On 5 January 1895, in the courtyard of the École Militaire in Paris, Captain Alfred Dreyfus was being 'formally degraded' before silent ranks of soldiers – by having the rank insignia, buttons and braid cut from his uniform and his sword broken – while a large crowd of onlookers shouted abuse from behind railings. This process, also known as 'cashiering', was at the time the French army custom for dismissing officers for gross misconduct.

Dreyfus, a French Jew, had been found guilty of treason. He was subsequently exonerated and it is now widely considered that anti-Semitism had a role in his conviction. Dreyfus later described this experience as a 'horrible torture', in far more emotional language than he described his subsequent incarceration, and wrote to his wife:

> My torn, dishonoured garments would bring me brutally back to reality. The looks of hate and scorn told me, only too plainly, why I was there [...] How well I understand them! In their place I could not have restrained my contempt for an officer branded a traitor to his country. But alas! Here is the pitiful tragedy. There is a traitor, but it is not I![16]

This is a visible and painful example of rejection from a group – or ostracism. What is particularly striking about Dreyfus' account is that it is clear he still identified with the group that was rejecting him and he desired inclusion: he believed that cashiering, and the shame that came with it, was the appropriate punishment for someone guilty of the crime of which he has been convicted.

We imagine Dreyfus would agree with the description of ostracism as the 'social death penalty',[17] but not all rejection is as acute as Dreyfus' humiliation, or even Michael's disastrous job interview. Imagine you're playing a game with two other people, tossing a ball to one another. What if the others stopped tossing it to you? The first couple of times you might think it's just chance, but pretty quickly it starts to feel like rejection: you've been pushed out of the game.

Studies find ostracism from this game (measured by percentage of throws in which the 'ball' is passed to the player) takes a significant toll on both interpersonal (aggression, kindness) and intrapersonal (self-esteem, emotions) measures.[18] Interestingly, the immediate effects of this rejection are the same regardless of whether it's by a group that we consider ourselves a member of, a group we don't consider ourselves a member of (such as members of a different political party to ours), another group that we might find repellent (like members of the Ku Klux Klan) or even a computer.[19]

The explanation the study favours for this is that rejection is so painful that it overwhelms considerations of who is doing the rejecting. However, another interpretation has to do with which social groups are most relevant to us at the moment when we're being ostracized. It's possible that when playing the ball-tossing game the identity that's most salient to us in that moment is to 'people playing this game', temporarily supplanting the wider social groups of 'white supremacist' and 'not a white supremacist'. With that identity at the front of our mind, it hurts when our fellow game-players reject us, even if in another context we'd want nothing to do with them.

Starting a new job, especially a stressful or demanding one, can be nerve-wracking. In the first days and weeks, our main concern is often whether or not we'll fit in with other members of the group. A female friend of ours recounted how after being in a group task with three other candidates – all of them men – and then being interviewed by an all-male panel she resolved to turn down a job offer if she received one because it seemed like the organization was the kind of place that would be dominated by more male stereotypes, and therefore she wouldn't fit in. In the event, she did receive a job offer and she did decline it. In this instance, the group didn't reject her; but she felt that even if they were prepared to accept her professionally she wouldn't be socially accepted – and she was neither willing nor able to change herself enough to conform to what she perceived the expectations of that group to be.

Feeling like you're going to be accepted into the group is likely to be particularly important in professions like nursing or teaching, which are stressful but generally not well paid and consequently can be less highly regarded by some. As such, belongingness and social support within the profession are likely more important than they would be for, say, stockbrokers. Accordingly, one would expect people in these professions to try harder to avoid rejection through conformity and internalization of group values.

One study looked at student nurses undertaking their clinical placements, to gauge how they sought to fit in with the registered nurses at the hospital, and found that the nursing students would avoid 'rocking the boat' – for example by raising issues like the nurses using outdated or banned practice[20] – because their main priority was to be accepted into the group. Students who already felt accepted were more willing to raise instances of outdated practice – but, as the authors of that study point out, the nursing profession has tried to move away from 'conformity, subservience, uniformity and compliance', out of a recognition that trying to avoid rocking the boat can actually cost lives.

Some of our sense of belonging to a group, and the self-esteem that comes with that, stems from whether we view ourselves as a good member of the group – in other words, how closely we fit with the stereotype of the social groups we value. As a result, we may be reluctant to undertake actions that are inconsistent with that stereotype, or might move us away from the 'ideal' for that group, even if in a larger sense those actions would benefit us. For instance, one piece of research found that for African-American students in mixed schools, there is a negative relationship between academic achievement and popularity that does not exist for white students, and which is stronger the more racially diverse the school is.[21] There is an argument that these students face a trade-off between investing in education and being seen as invested in peer groups and their community.[22]

In the UK, the analogue is not young black students;[23] it's white working-class boys, who are afraid not of acting white but of acting 'posh', with the same underlying insecurity that by investing in education a student is signalling that they plan to leave their peer groups and their communities. The bullying and mocking that come from acting above one's station, of daring to display the affectation of studying hard, make it harder for young people from these backgrounds to succeed academically.

Researchers find that it's the people who think their own position in the group is weakest and most vulnerable that are both the most keen to conform – to strengthen their position – and to actively and aggressively police the norms of the group when others break the rules.

If other group members may turn on us when we break the norms of the group, how do we respond to internal threats to our identity when we ourselves act in a way that's inconsistent with our identity, moving us (if only in our own minds) away from the ideal?

Compensating like this can be seen in how we behave as consumers. A recent study found that when people have to buy something that is inconsistent with their identity (for instance, a Tottenham supporter buying Chelsea merchandise for a friend's birthday) they tended to try to 'balance it out' (by buying more Tottenham gear, or cheering extra loud at the next game, or writing something rude about Chelsea in the accompanying card). [24]

But what about times when we're aware of a stereotype about our group that we don't want to conform to, and might actively reject? You've probably seen an ad that equates cleaning your house to being a princess in a fairy tale, or being Wonder Woman, or being a good mother. Delightful, aren't they?

Now, take a look at the maths problems below. See if you can figure out the answers.

1. At what point does the line $2x - y = 4$ cross the y-axis?
2. What kind of function is this: $f(X) = \sqrt[3]{(x - 1)}$?
3. What is the value of t if: $3x^2 + tx - 21 = (3x - 3)(x + 7)$?
4. What is $110 \div 4$? *

These maths questions are at roughly the level taught to sixteen-year-olds in the UK. Perhaps you found them difficult, or perhaps enough maths came back to you that you managed to take a stab at a couple. Or perhaps you thought, 'It's too early/late/sunny outside

---

* Answers are 1. (0,-4); 2. A cube-root function; 3. 18; 4. 27.5.

to do maths,' and skimmed straight down to this paragraph

But for some readers, something else might have gone on as well. Particularly, in this case, for those readers who fit into the social category of (white) woman. Here, your ability to get to grips with these questions may have been affected by the awareness that you are part of a group often considered to be weak at maths. When this happens, it's what researchers call a *stereotype threat*. The threat manifests as a fixation, or over-attentiveness, on the negative stereotype itself, which distracts us from the task at hand.

The idea behind stereotype threat is quite simple, but its effects are surprisingly powerful. This form of identity threat is made more likely when membership of that social group is brought front and centre – for example, by a heavily gendered advertisement for cleaning products.

In the modern day, this kind of negative stereotype leads to the same threat response as other social threats. Unfortunately, in a maths exam, neither flight nor fight are good options and focusing on the negative stereotype doesn't help us to overcome it.

Even if we won't admit it, almost all of us can relate to that feeling in an exam when our heart races and we begin to perspire, unable to think beyond what will happen if we fail. In our adult lives, we get the same situation when we can't get to sleep and find ourselves overheating in bed in mid-December, fixating on that big presentation tomorrow and what will happen if it goes wrong. Stereotype threat takes this up a notch – it's not just 'What will people think of me?' but also 'What if the stereotype is right?'

Stereotype threat gets worse. Think back to those sleepless nights. How many times have you told yourself to calm down, to 'just go to sleep' – because it is after all a big day tomorrow? How much good has that done you? This is the third component of stereotype threat: because you know it's not helpful, you fruitlessly spend more energy trying to suppress your initial response to the threat.

The effects of stereotype threat on both how we approach opportunities to do well in life and our access to such opportunities are substantial, although exactly how substantial is a matter of debate. However, it's really an issue only when we're looking to break free of a stereotype about our group, or deviate from a particular group norm. We know that deviating from the group is painful, either because of how we're treated by other members of the group, or because of a loss of our own self-esteem. Most of the time, we'll try to avoid that pain by changing our behaviour to be more consistent with the norms of the group.

Our desire to conform means that our behaviour when we're acting as a member of a group is sometimes different from how it would be when we act as an individual. We might adhere more closely to a group decision, even if our own judgement suggests it's not a good idea; and we can do things – from lying to cheating or even committing murder – because we're following others in the group or protecting the group's interests.

We use our social groups, and our sense of which behaviours are in keeping with them, to justify a multitude of sins when we think (or at least can convince ourselves) that our group membership gives us licence to behave in ways we know to be wrong or inappropriate.

A revealing set of studies explored whether a shared social group identification could 'license' students to cheat.[25] A group of students were brought together and asked to complete a difficult maths task. The students then self-marked their answers, gave the researcher their overall score, received compensation based on the number of questions they'd answered correctly and then shredded their test sheet, signifying that they would not be caught if they lied about their score. But, in fact, the shredder did not shred, and the researchers were able to compare the number of correct answers the student claimed with their actual performance.

About sixty seconds after the task began, a confederate stood up, said he got everything right, shredded his paper and claimed the money. It would have been clear to other participants that this person must have cheated. But in the two conditions there was a key difference: in one, the confederate wore a plain T-shirt; in the other, the confederate wore a T-shirt from a rival university. What the researchers wanted to know was whether participants would engage in more riskless cheating when they saw a fellow student do it, with whom they shared a salient social group, than when a rival student did it. Compared to the group where there was no confederate, seeing a fellow student cheat significantly increased cheating, while significantly fewer students cheated when they saw a student from a rival university cheat.

This 'licence' to behave in particular ways, when others like us are doing it and we perceive no consequences, can help to explain why 'bad' people appear to be much more common in times of crisis than they are when things are going smoothly. It may also help us to understand the seeming disconnect between the kind and normal people we meet every day, and the actions of large groups.

Building strong identities and asking us to behave as a member of that identity group is fairly standard fare for the world's militaries. An army at war could not function without a large number of people who are willing to do something that they would never normally do in civilian life – attack and kill others;

sometimes people from another group but often, in the case of a civil war, people who were recently friends and neighbours. Psychopaths, whose lack of a moral centre lets them kill without remorse, are hard to find. Even if you could find enough, an army of psychopaths would lack cohesion and a willingness to die for a cause.

Instead, armies create soldiers and a strong identity based on three foundations: shared values, shared experiences and uniformity in both behaviour and attire. Rhonda Cornum, a retired US army general who was a prisoner of war during the first Gulf War and later went on to develop the US armed forces' resilience-training programme, argues that we shouldn't expect people's psychology to change when they put on an army uniform. Cornum argues that the US army should take better care of its soldiers' mental wellbeing and not assume that they have infinite stores of mental or physical stamina. She is indisputably right about this, but perhaps overstates things: putting on a uniform, and assuming that identity of 'soldier', combined with their training, does seem to make soldiers capable of doing some things that the rest of us would not.

Many of these things are astonishing in a good way – running protracted distances while carrying heavy packs, bravery in the face of extreme danger and a willingness to sacrifice yourself for the group. Some are more ambiguous – killing other people, even in self-defence, is not really a positive thing, but it'd be hard to argue that it isn't an essential part of maintaining an effective army. And sometimes belonging to the army leads people to be capable of things that are quite beyond their usual boundaries, and certainly negative. For hundreds of years, atrocities committed by invading armies have been excused away as the 'spoils of war' or 'just following orders'. These were just the kinds of things that soldiers did, even if hardly any of them would do the same in civilian life.

Our social instincts, which tell us to stay part of the group – even if that means conforming, self-censoring or punishing others – can clearly produce undesirable results and quite by accident, without us even knowing. Combined with the discrimination we saw in Chapter 1, this paints quite a bleak picture of our social selves, whose instincts lead us, seemingly inexorably, down a path to doubting ourselves and bullying everyone else – whether they're friends or foes.

The social influences on our behaviour are more powerful now than ever before, and the availability of data and quite a lot of ill intent has enabled the manipulation of the social environment. We are increasingly being led to undesirable outcomes not by accident but by design: social influence has moved from an art to a science, recasting much of the world as we know it.

3

Manipulation

'Humans say the road to hell is paved with good intentions. Why? Do they think there's a shortage of bad ones?'

Andromeda, Gene Roddenberry

LESS THAN A year before Northern Rock was nationalized and the bank queues piled up, people around the world were queuing around the block for a very different reason. On 29 June 2007, Apple launched the iPhone. For younger readers, it's perhaps hard to understand the changes that the iPhone brought about. Smartphones had existed before this but the market was dominated by the Blackberry, which while being very … functional, was really a sexy product only to a class of largely middle-aged, largely male business people for whom (it could be said) it provided an additional reason to ignore their families by replying to emails at all times of the day and night.

The iPhone continued where the Blackberry had started, to put our means of working and communicating in our pockets. But it went – and continues to go – further. Without an iPhone or the smartphone takeover it precipitated, we would have (for example) no Uber – no ability to instantaneously summon a cab to take us exactly where we want to go at the touch of a button.

We'd have (even) less control of our finances, and we'd not be able to book a holiday while idly waiting for a bus.

The rise of wearable technology like Fitbits would not have been possible without smartphones, or would have certainly travelled much more slowly. We wouldn't have been able to hastily edit documents while walking to meetings, or order a drink to be brought to our seat at the theatre without even standing up. And our understanding of the conflict between (angry) birds and pigs would be much less advanced.

Even these momentous strides forward for human happiness are dwarfed, however, by another change – the arrival of the modern social network. From its CEO Mark Zuckerberg's dorm room to world domination, Facebook spread from elite institution to elite institution before eventually allowing anyone and everyone to sign up. When the social network arrived at a college it almost invariably spread like wildfire, transforming the social life of the campus.

Facebook hasn't obviously changed the fundamentals of our social selves, but it has taken existing phenomena to a new level. As Jesse Eisenberg, playing Zuckerberg, says in the film *The Social Network*: 'People want to go on the internet and check out their friends … pictures, profiles, whatever you can … visit, browse around, maybe it's somebody you just met at a party … talking about taking the entire social experience of college and putting it online … This is what drives life at college. Are you having sex or aren't you? It's why people take certain classes, and sit where they sit, and do what they do, and at its centre, you know, that's what the Facebook is gonna be about.' In the public domain, Facebook became not only the way that we organized our social lives but also a valuable tool for procrastination – had anyone posted to your wall? How many people were coming to your event? However, while still confined to computers that were immobile, bulky, or had a short battery life, there was a limit to the network's reach.

The arrival of smartphones, and in particular the widespread use of them by young people and students, let Facebook off the leash to enjoy the ubiquity it has today. In 2019, it remains the dominant social networking platform, with more than 2 billion users globally – but it is not alone. If we want to brag about our lives to (or be bragged at by) people we know, Facebook remains the top of the tree. If you want to argue with total strangers about politics, or find out the innermost thoughts of the President of the United States, Twitter's the platform for you. If you want to be disheartened about the aesthetic state of your diet by thousands of photos of friends, famous people or anyone in between,* Instagram has got your back.

Like Facebook, none of these new platforms have transformed our psychology, but they have allowed our social instincts to run wild, with more information, and more points of comparison, available at the touch of a button.

This is by and large not a bad thing – in moderation. But problems start to creep in when our social instincts – to look around, to try to learn from what we see and to compare ourselves to others – are unleashed in a new environment online. Our desire for social information and interaction keeps driving us back for more.

In the seventeenth century, Louis XIV of France built the Palace at Versailles as a way of keeping an eye on his troublesome

---

* (and their dogs)

nobles. If you wanted to have access to the king, you had to live at Versailles: crammed into tiny rooms; living on top of your friends, enemies and lovers every minute of every day; waiting for your chance to watch the king getting dressed. It was, by all accounts, miserable: a hyper-competitive, rule-bound, surreal existence. By absorbing his nobles with ritual and scandal, Louis ensured they'd have no time to get in his way. Although a lot has changed in the world since the Sun King's time, there are some aspects of life at court that may seem a little familiar to us now.

In 2017, a survey by the professional-services company Deloitte found that 38 per cent of adults say they use their phones too much – 56 per cent among people aged sixteen to twenty-four.[26] If you take into account people's tendency to reflect on their own behaviour in a flattering light, and the increasing ubiquity of smartphones (in 2017–18, 85 per cent of people in the UK[27] and 77 per cent of people in the US[28] owned a smartphone, up from 52 per cent and 35 per cent respectively in 2011) then the true figure in 2019 is probably higher and on the rise. And the single largest use of time on smartphones is on social media.

Each of these social media platforms is successful because it taps into some aspect of our social instincts. And it is the insatiability of the same instincts that Louis XIV played upon to control his courtiers centuries earlier that can hook us in. For example, we can't control our instinct to look for comparison, and research by Harvard Business School professor Ashley Whillans suggests that we consistently assume that other people are more socially connected than us,[29] leaving us scrabbling for more friends, more likes, more connections, to keep up with the pack – which is itself suffering the same worries.

In previous chapters we've seen what group membership can do in justifying bad behaviour, and even eliciting more of it. We've also seen how our social instincts can run wild with the myriad connections made possible by technology. If this is what can happen when we are simply pulled about by the naturally occurring tides of social influence, what would happen if someone tried to harness that power – and succeeded in doing so?

Attempts to manipulate people using their social identities are nothing new. For example, on both sides of the Second World War and later the Cold War, propaganda rose to an art form, encouraging suspicion of the other side.

In the twenty-first century, with all its technology and data, people and organizations who want to influence you have moved beyond art and into the domain of science.

To a certain extent, if Facebook, Twitter and Instagram can't manipulate you, they're in trouble. This is because their business model relies on being able to sell users' attention to people who want to sell those users other products. If people buy more Diet Coke because they've seen an advert for Diet Coke on Twitter, or seen that their Facebook friends like Diet Coke, then the Coca-Cola Company might be willing to pay Twitter to advertise their product, or to pay Facebook to roll out a social media strategy that wins their product more 'likes'.

This is something Facebook has devoted a lot of research time to. After all, being able to reach a large audience and influence people is the reason that Facebook's true customers – advertisers – use the platform. Research carried out on Facebook has looked at whether or not the things that you like or share on Facebook influence the behaviour of other people in your network,[30] and whether it matters how involved you were in that process – if Facebook shares the things you like only with your networks, is that less effective than if you choose what is shared and what isn't?[31]

In these studies, the influence of everyday behaviours existed but was small, and people didn't seem to respond more as they saw more shares from the same person. Perhaps we are willing to go only so far in demonstrating our similarity to our friends.

Since our behaviour online can influence those around us, Facebook's engineers got to thinking about what else it could do beyond just providing us with a sense of what our friends from college were up to, organizing parties and selling us new goods and services. Could it be used to encourage us to be better citizens?

Facebook's internal researchers put this to the test in the 2010 Congressional Elections in the US with 61 million Americans, aged over eighteen, who visited Facebook on the day of the election.[32] Most (about 60 million) of those people were randomly chosen to be shown a social message that encouraged them to vote, told them how many people had voted so far (at least, how many people had told Facebook they had voted so far), and showed them a picture of six of their Facebook friends who had already said they'd voted.

People who saw this message were compared with two other groups – an information group who saw everything other than the pictures of their Facebook friends, and a control group who didn't see any of the information. Analysing publicly available data on whether someone actually voted, researchers found no effect at all – precisely 0 of the informational message – compared to the control group. Being encouraged by Facebook to vote, and knowing how many people had told Facebook they were voting, didn't influence voting behaviour.[33] But when people saw the faces of their own friends who had reportedly voted, this did have an effect – increasing the likelihood of somebody voting by 0.39 per cent points.

This doesn't sound like a lot – close to a rounding error – but with Facebook's enormous reach it adds up fast. And the effect doesn't stop there. When people who saw the message voted, they could share the face on their own wall – to show their friends that they'd taken part more directly – posting a digital version of the 'I voted' stickers that are given out at US elections.[34]

Today is Election Day   What's this? • close

Find your polling place on the U.S.   0 1 1 5 5 3 7 6
Politics Page and click the "I Voted"   People on Facebook Voted
button to tell your friends you voted.

I Voted

 🅕 Jaime Settle, Jason Jones, and 18 other
friends have voted.

The effects here are also small – for each 'close' friend that a person had who was in the 'faces' treatment group, they themselves became 0.22 per cent more likely to vote (more remote friends had no impact). But the effects compound the more close friends you've got that see the message, and the average user has ten close friends.[35] Taken together, these interventions increased the number of votes by 340,000 nationally in the 2010 election.

As a first attempt by Facebook at driving election participation, it was pretty powerful; and it didn't take a lot at the time for political operatives to start thinking about how this could be used in future. A uniform spread of 340,000 across the US wouldn't have a big impact on anything – but if it could be targeted, that would be a whole different story: 340,000 votes is more than the combined Republican majority in the 2016 presidential election in Michigan, Wisconsin, Pennsylvania, Alaska, Arizona and Florida, whose eighty-nine electoral college votes between them would have turned Donald Trump's victory into a landslide for the Democrats.[36]

Even perfectly deployed to Republican voters in small or marginal states (New Hampshire, Nevada, Florida and Ohio), these 340,000 voters couldn't overturn the 2012 presidential election that returned

President Obama to the White House, but it would be enough to shrink the margin of victory to just five electoral college votes.

So, as Facebook were flying high on their ability to encourage civic engagement and make the world a better place, working out how to harness the power of their platform was rising rapidly to the list of priorities for political parties, public relations groups and lobbyists.

On the other side of Facebook's research agenda, the company was focusing on the negative side of sharing, and one that they'd realized was becoming ever more important: the spread of inaccurate information.

Back in 2014, a team of researchers turned their attention to 'rumour cascades' on Facebook: the way that demonstrably false information spreads through networks, mostly through 'memes' – messages or images copied and pasted into multiple feeds, often with minimal modification. To do this (and to save having to work out true from false) they identified any threads of things shared on Facebook into which another user at some point shared a link from the popular rumour-debunking site Snopes identifying that the story shared was false. From the point of the Snopes article being linked, they were then able to trace back the history of the post to see where it originated – and who else had shared it – producing network diagrams like the one shown in the image below.[37]

We can think of the network as a tree emanating from a single initial point, or seed, with each person sharing creating a new branch. Some branches will die quickly – if posted by someone without many friends or much influence, perhaps, while others will go far, spurring a number of additional shares. Each of those secondary shares in turn creates its own branch, which can either die immediately or be shared more widely.

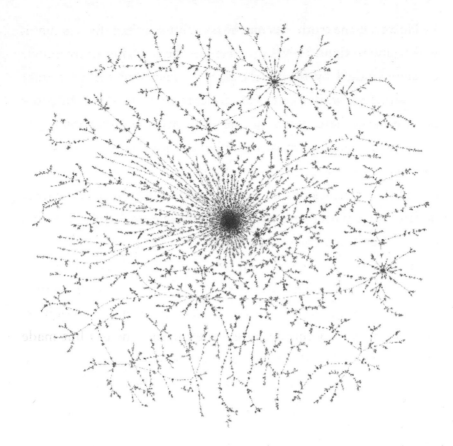

Each branch of the cascade forms when someone shares a false story, and then branches again when someone in their network shares it, and so on.

Using this kind of analysis, the Facebook researchers could identify how far false rumours could spread, and what happened when other people tried to stop them in their tracks by posting a refutation.

They found that the networks of rumours spread quickly, but also that the rate at which a refutation worked was faster than you might think – on average within about ten minutes. When people saw a refutation had been posted, it seemed to be pretty effective at stopping or slowing the rate of the rumour growing – seemingly good news for those of us who want to see the truth triumph over lies.

However, the truth was much less common than the lies that it was trying to fight: only 15 per cent of the branches of a rumour cascade studied by the Facebook researchers led to an attempt at debunking, while the remainder carried on unchecked. More depressing is the problem of selection, because Facebook's way of knowing that a tree was spreading a false rumour was that someone posted a Snopes link to refute it at some point on at least one of the branches of that tree. We don't know how many trees of false information still exist where no one even tried to refute the falsehood.

If refutation is effective but limited, could fighting fire with fire work? Could memes prove to be an effective weapon against memes? To test this, they looked at the effectiveness of counter-memes – messages that parodied the original memes but made fun of the people daft enough to fall for them. The researchers found that in most cases, counter-memes were ineffective, with hardly any of the same momentum and power of the initial, false, meme.[38]

Each instance of untruth – be it a satirist passing for a real journalist at the end of his tether, as in the case of the British character 'Jonathan Pie', or a meme indicating that Facebook is about to start charging for access to the platform, or will start using your data for nefarious purposes unless you repost it – isn't necessarily damaging to our overall sense of truth. However, the volume of the untruths, and the speed with which they spread, undermines our ability to learn from the social environment.

This is partly, as we've seen, just a consequence of the online social media environment – the cost of doing business on a platform like Twitter or Facebook. However, it could also, in part, be down to the deliberate actions of some people and organizations.

This is the contention of the anthropologist Alexei Yurchak, who studied the collapse of the Soviet Union and who argues that the successful spread of propaganda in the USSR had the effect of creating two parallel realities for citizens: one, the real world, in which they encountered a daily struggle, queuing for hours for the necessities of life; and another, the product of the relentless propaganda of the Soviet Union, in which the harsh reality was refuted and went unexpressed, first in public and then in private and finally even within the confines of their own heads.

When this 'hypernormalization', as Yurchak calls it, takes hold, we can't conceive of an alternative to it – just as Russians could not conceive, at the time, an alternative to the Soviet Union even as it was clearly failing, and so were surprised by its eventual rapid collapse. This kind of mass delusion, according to British documentary filmmaker Adam Curtis, now grips the West. Leaders have created simplistic narratives to explain our world and what happens in it, and which we in turn have absorbed, believed and shared, creating a similar mass delusion about the way the world is.

By way of example, Curtis in his 2016 documentary *HyperNormalisation* points to the emergence of Colonel Qaddafi, then leader of Libya, as a powerful global enemy of the West and its values in the 1980s. In this construction, Qaddafi, who was not popular among other Arab leaders at the time, was either a patsy on whom the American intelligence services could blame the world's ills as a common enemy, or a self-aggrandizing maniac who was all too happy to burnish his own status by accepting responsibility – which in turn led to him being able to actually support terrorism. Curtis applies this argument across the gamut of world events, arguing that the reluctance of leaders to make

difficult decisions and to wrestle with the complexity of the world
has led them to create false narratives to guide the public towards
a simple narrative that we're prone to accepting.

What might previously have been dismissed as the domain of
conspiracy theorists has become much harder to ignore in recent
years, as the sheer volume of falsehoods has reached a state of
seeming ubiquity, particularly surrounding the Brexit referendum
and the 2016 US presidential election.

The emergence of 'fake news' was one of the driving narratives
of both these democratic exercises. The accusation that Hillary
Clinton and the Democrats had sought to cover up a Washington,
DC paedophile ring was just one of thousands of examples, and
that seems to have been the point. Increasing evidence, gathered by
both US and British intelligence services, suggests that our social
selves are being hijacked to destabilize our society and to destroy
our trust that what we read on the internet is true.

A growing consensus among security services and law-
enforcement agencies holds that Facebook and Twitter accounts
run by Russian intelligence services were responsible for
beginning wave after wave of false content on social media.
Most of the accounts that are posting fake news have very few
or perhaps even no 'real' followers – rather, many of them exist
in a kind of shadow social network of their own. But they post
these stories and like, re-share and retweet them repeatedly.
Eventually they break through into the networks of real people.
Someone sees a post that's just about believable, and doesn't
challenge their pre-existing beliefs, and they see that it's already
been shared several times (by other 'trolls') – and they share
it themselves. After a certain point, it becomes difficult to tell
whether a new piece of information is true or false – and so we

end up believing that everything is at least in part a lie, and that nothing can be trusted.

This came to the fore after the EU referendum. Russian trolls, apparently supporting the Leave campaign, posted fake news stories talking down the Remain campaign, overstating the benefits of leaving the European Union and the ills that came with membership. Concerned about this, and the risk to the economy of leaving the EU, the civil service took an unprecedented step of writing to every residence in the country to lay out the findings of the Treasury's economic impact assessment.

The British civil service, for all their caricature at the hands of TV shows like *Yes Minister* and *The Thick of It*, are a professional civil service whose code requires them to serve the government of the day without fear or favour but prohibits them from getting involved in party-political matters. The Brexit impact assessments, which were carried out in that spirit, are what is called 'conditional forecasts' – a form of economic forecasting that is the stock in trade for economists and which, unlike unconditional forecasts, have a good track record of accuracy.

Unconditional forecasts aim to say, for example, 'How much will shares in Microsoft be worth on 1 April 2025?', and to provide an estimate for the level of those shares – let's say £15. Because of the number of things that can affect share prices – the weather, failed product launches, bad investments, the activity of rival firms, and so on – this estimate isn't going to be very accurate. Extrapolate up to the level of an entire economy, and things look even more complicated.

A conditional forecast, by contrast, doesn't aim to tell us exactly what's going to happen – just how different two possible futures are likely to be based on only one thing changing: for example,

If Rand's research, though still in its early stages, offers a ray of sunshine into a bleak landscape, we have already upon us a far greater abuse of our social selves for which we currently have no defence: direct and targeted manipulation of the information that we see to get us to move our behaviour in a particular direction.

An important part of any social media platform is the pruning and tweaking of our feeds – working out which handful of posts among thousands to give prominence in the news feeds, or which tweets to put in your 'in case you missed it' selection when you haven't checked in for a while. Platform owners must decide which posts to promote or highlight and which ones not to, and there is no natural or neutral way to do this. They could promote the posts most likely to encourage you to return to the platform – perhaps by playing on your need for social comparison by highlighting the 'Amazing holiday in Barbados #blessed' pictures and the 'Pleased to say I've got the promotion!!' posts rather than 'Another standard day at the office'. Or they could choose the posts most likely to encourage you to buy something from one of the platform's advertisers – positioning pictures of appetizing food alongside adverts for local restaurants, maybe. These, the two most obvious options, face trade-offs: the more promotional posts you see, the more valuable advertising revenue is; but the more addicted you are to the platform, the easier it will be to advertise to you later.

Platforms can also choose to prioritize feeds in other, creepier ways. In 2014, Facebook undertook an experiment that for many users and commentators reached new heights of creepiness, even from a platform built to allow people to overshare personal information. The experiment was simple: some users were chosen at random to see disproportionately more 'happy' posts by their friends, while others saw the feed as usual and a third group saw relatively more negative posts. It turned out that there were modest but real effects on people's own posts, which got happier the happier their feed was. When this study became public knowledge there was a huge backlash against Facebook for conducting this kind of research, or for daring to try to manipulate the emotions of their users in this way – sufficient criticism to prompt Facebook to dramatically rein in its research operations. But by this point the word was out: your emotions could be manipulated through social media platforms.

The Russian government's tactic of flooding us with fake news lacks subtlety and indeed was quickly picked up on, both during and after the elections it was being used to influence. A subtler approach involves looking at our social exhaust: that is, all the information we put about ourselves online – all of our tweets, likes, photos, geolocations – as well as demographic information and the answers we give to surveys. Essentially our digital social fingerprint.

Using a combination of this exhaust and modern statistical techniques (as well as other survey data harvested with dubious legality) was exactly what the confusingly named London-based company Cambridge Analytica did. During the 2016 presidential election, Cambridge Analytica, whose executives included Steve Bannon, formerly chief strategist to President Donald Trump, gathered data on users and used machine learning to identify their 'type' – essentially creating a rich profile of their likely hopes and dreams, their political leanings and the kinds of advertising to which they were likely to be the most or least responsive.

The data, some of which was harvested illegally in 2015 from some 50 million Facebook users, was used to 'exploit what we knew about them and target their inner demons', in the words of Christopher Wylie, a former Cambridge Analytica employee turned whistleblower.[40] The goal was clear: to feed potential Trump voters the types of adverts that played into their identities and fears, to get them most likely to vote their way, while feeding likely Clinton voters adverts that suppressed that voting instinct or at very least failed to mobilize them. This is perhaps the most sophisticated attempt to interfere in an election ever seen.

After this became public thanks to investigative reporters, Facebook faced a new backlash from which it is still trying to rehabilitate itself. The police raided Cambridge Analytica and seized their data, leading the company ultimately to shut down. It is possible – although unconfirmed as we write this – that authorities in the US or the UK will charge Cambridge Analytica's employees and directors with a crime. Either way, the use of harvested data in this way casts a long shadow, leading many to wonder whether the power of social media to influence us has grown too large and too hard to control.

At this stage, it's hard not to be sympathetic to this argument. Cambridge Analytica shut down in May 2018; prior to that, in March of that year, Alexander Nix, its CEO during the 2016 election, was suspended. There is nothing to stop Nix, or others like him, from starting again in a new company that could sell their election-manipulation services to the highest bidder – with the Cambridge Analytica scandal serving as free advertising for such a venture. In fact, Nix was appointed as a director of a new company, Emerdata, in January 2018, along with Julian Wheatland, the chairman of Cambridge Analytica's parent company, and Alexander Taylor, Cambridge Analytica's chief data officer.

The ability of the manipulators themselves to evade the authorities by shutting up shop and reopening elsewhere may explain why the focus of politicians' ire has been directed at the platforms and at Facebook in particular. Mark Zuckerberg was summoned before the UK parliament, the US Congress and the European parliament. Having refused to appear before the Brits, and in doing so providing more ammunition to critics who suspect that Facebook believes itself above the law, Zuckerberg at least turned up for Congress and the Europeans, where he appeared before the elected representatives of the two largest economies in the world, who asked such hard-hitting questions as 'How do you sustain a business model in which users don't pay for your service?'[41] and 'Is Twitter the same as what you do?'

Zuckerberg answered questions for days and seems to have come out on top, albeit apologizing for Facebook's failure to protect its users' data and for not telling them when it had previously been stolen. If we think that the purpose of the hearings was something more than theatre, more than political point-scoring, then there are no winners. Facebook, despite its power, feels threatened enough to put adverts out in the real world bearing such truisms as 'Fake news is not your friend', but politicians and their governments seem unable to understand what Facebook is, much less how it can influence the world around it and how that could be effectively regulated.

This is hardly surprising. Banks as institutions are millennia old and we've still not cracked how to regulate them. The difference is that banks' ability to influence politics is actually fairly limited and easy to trace. The last few years have shown us that our social selves, unleashed by the internet and social media, can undermine the democratic institutions of our society in ways that are hard to

detect and that muddy the already murky waters of democracy. We don't know what the future holds, or even how powerful these techniques actually are (Cambridge Analytica and Russian trolls aren't publishing their findings), but even relatively modest manipulation can have outsized impact.

We've seen how our social selves, and social media, can steer us in a particular direction without us realizing, and how we can fall prey to perils because of the social environment and our own social instincts. In the case of Facebook, but also more broadly, governments using traditional tools, and traditional ways of thinking about citizens' lives and decision-making, are vulnerable to the tides that this creates and, like King Canute, powerless to turn them back.[42]

In Part 2, we're going to begin to take a more positive approach, and tell a story of social influence that sometimes struggles to break through at the moment. The history of human beings is one of interaction between people. Without these interactions, and the instincts that give rise ot them, we would never have flourished as a species.

Talk of a social influence induced cataclysm, threatening to undermine our societies, holds some weight, but around this dismal picture lurks thousands of silver linings. For example, while the use of social media in an election can be harmful, it has also helped to enfranchise and engage a wider group of voters. For all the ways in which our social groups can be cliquey and discriminatory, they can also rally around us when things get tough. Like when flooding hit the UK a few years ago; we saw the social instincts of people dozens of miles away kicking in when they opened their doors to those who had lost their homes – offering everything from laundry to temporary accommodation.

If our newspapers are filled with horror stories of social influence, our daily lives contain lots of small social acts that make our lives better. The important question now is therefore how can we harness our social instincts to benefit ourselves, as well as those around us?

PART 2

Nudges

4

Social Groups

'Everything may be labelled – but everybody is not.'

The Age of Innocence, Edith Wharton

O N A CHILLY day in November 1913, a crowd gathered in Hartford, Connecticut. There was a great deal of anticipation in the air; the speaker was a legend, who had travelled from Britain to raise support for what had become her life's project. When she stepped on stage, people observed that she was small, very slim and fashionably dressed. She was a married woman, with three daughters.

And then she began to speak: 'I do not come here as an advocate ... I am here as a soldier who has temporarily left the field of battle.' A startling statement from one who was the image of Edwardian femininity.

The speaker was Emmeline Pankhurst, and she had a mission: justifying the actions her Women's Social and Political Union had taken in the name of women's suffrage, through the construction of a form of feminine identity that was political and militant. Her choice of clothing was deliberate, as was her use of phrases such as 'We women' and 'We wear no mark; we belong to every class.'

She must have been aware that for this to work it was vital that the women to whom she spoke first identified her as being part of 'their' group. If they did, perhaps they would start to see the similarities between Pankhurst and themselves and see the sense in what she was saying. If they did not, they would leave unconvinced and hostile, dismissing her as a frenzied suffragette and not one of them.

This is an example of a shared identity used to mobilize people towards a powerful good: a stronger, more representative democracy.

Indeed, social identity theorists argue that sense of a shared social group is the basis for social influence and organization.[43] When people perceive themselves to share group membership with another person in a given context they not only expect to agree with that person on issues relevant to their shared identity but are also motivated to strive actively to reach agreement and to co-ordinate their behaviour in relation to those issues on which they disagree. For instance, at work, if we strongly identify with our team, or with the company, then that motivation to reach agreement can make people go the extra mile.

Social identity starts with us identifying with particular social groups, and associating with the groups that we've put ourselves in, often at a pretty deep level. Doing this helps us create and define our place in the social environment, understand ourselves and others in terms of these groups and act according to our group membership.[44]

The process of group identification is broadly as follows:[45]

1. We self-categorize into a particular group (social identity theory requires this categorization to be consensual: it's not enough that others might categorize Michael as an eccentric

based on his collection of bow ties; he must also categorize himself as an eccentric – which he does);

2. We start to see ourselves as being closer to and having more in common with other members of this group; and

3. We seek to 'positively differentiate' the group we have affiliated with – by highlighting the things that make our group special, better or more desirable than other groups – because this positive differentiation increases our self-esteem and positive self-concept.

So, seeing the world through our social groups means that we self-categorize into a group, move closer psychologically to other members of the group and seek to positively differentiate the group from others. For instance, we might self-categorize as woman or man, cyclist, cat or dog person, *Star Wars* fan, alumnus of our university, and so on. These groups can be small and interactive – like families and friendship groups – or large and general, associated with our characteristics. This instinct to self-categorize is a fundamental part of how we organize our experience of the world: we want to feel good about ourselves, and a positive image of ourselves based on our group membership is a profound motivator – to work harder, to collaborate more or to be more creative. When we encounter others in the same category we discover a kindred spirit.

We might expect a person's social groups to be straightforward to establish. Many people do indeed affiliate with social groups based on observable characteristics such as gender, ethnicity, nationality, sexuality and age. However, many don't and this makes identity much more complex than we might first imagine: for example, many people who were assigned female at birth do not identify themselves as being in the social category of 'woman'; they may have a different gender identity, feel that they don't comply (or don't wish to) with the stereotypical ideal of that identity, or may identify more strongly with an intersectional group such as 'black woman', 'lesbian woman', etc.

In addition, a great many of our self-perceived identities are connected not so much to demography as they are to values, behaviours or priorities we currently hold. For instance, Susannah has a WhatsApp group called 'Escape Force' in which a group of current and former BIT employees who are enthusiastic about escape rooms and other immersive puzzle games organize to go and try them out. The WhatsApp group chat provides the useful feature of being able to name chat groups, and as a result Susannah can refer to 'Escape Force' as opposed to 'that group of her friends and colleagues who like getting locked in themed rooms with time limits', but friends with shared interests and a shared identity are some of the most powerful social groups we can identify with.

The groups we're seeking to conform to even depend on the context we're in at the moment when the identity is called. Susannah was at a dinner party recently where the attendees didn't know each other very well, so decided to play a game where each person had to introduce themselves without using nouns or adjectives (this, by the way, is a difficult game). One of the attendees spent most of her time trying to figure out how to turn 'vegan' into a verb; she said that it was the first thing that came to her because she was surrounded by food at the time.

This introduces the concept of 'identity salience': which identity is front-of-mind in a particular situation, and how close to the front of our minds it is. Different social groups can be brought to the fore either by other people or by cues around us – making us alter the group we identify with in that moment.

Travellers abroad often spend a bit of time thinking about how they – as a result of their nationality – are distinct from locals or other travellers. Tourists from Britain and Australia complain loudly to each other about American tourists being brash and clueless, when of course not all American travellers are like this, and Brits and Australians hardly cover themselves in glory everywhere they go.

Susannah, before she joined the Behavioural Insights Team, worked in the Australian government and was used to describing herself as a 'public servant'[46] when talking to friends and colleagues who were lawyers, doctors, accountants, social workers and the like. But when she came to BIT, people frequently described themselves based on the academic discipline they had come from (with very friendly battle-lines drawn between the economists and the psychologists), so she started describing herself as a political scientist – something she'd never really done before except when trying to win arguments about politics.

Underpinning these processes is the constant development and negotiation of the 'ideal' member of the group. The ideal of the group is the set of characteristics and behaviours that exemplify the group to insiders: 'how we do things' and 'what makes us different'. People who deviate too far from the ideal may risk punishment or ostracism, as we heard about in Chapter 2. This was why Emmeline Pankhurst was so careful to dress fashionably and femininely, and why her small stature was a useful asset: it meant there was no visible basis on which to eject her from the social group of 'woman'. The group stereotype is the assumption (from group members and others) that all group members are the same and resemble the ideal.

The Harry Potter books (and, yes, the films too) provide an illustration of this. At the beginning of each year, all new first years at Hogwarts are arranged by the Sorting Hat into four houses:

Gryffindor, Hufflepuff, Ravenclaw and Slytherin. This is done partly based on how well the students fit the ideal of that house – the extent to which they are brave, hardworking, intellectual or ambitious – but also has an element of choice. Harry, having been underwhelmed by his encounter with ideal Slytherin Draco Malfoy, begs the Sorting Hat not to put him in Slytherin, so off to Gryffindor he goes. Over the series, we see through Harry's eyes the full range of interpersonal to intergroup behaviour: from his crush on Cho Chang, in which their different houses are barely relevant, to the Gryffindors' efforts to positively distinguish themselves from other houses, to the ultimate conflict between the Order of the Phoenix and the Death Eaters. In many cases, the individual differences between members of the same house are smoothed out in Harry's mind (and in readers' minds too) in favour of the group stereotype.

This social identification translates into the real world: it is possible to buy scarves, robes and T-shirts proclaiming affiliation to Hogwarts houses, and some of the stereotypes established in the fictional world of the books carry over to real life. Recently, there was a discussion among our colleagues at BIT about which Hogwarts house Michael would be in. Arguments were put forward that Michael could be a Gryffindor, Slytherin, Ravenclaw or even Hufflepuff, so Michael dutifully did the 'official' quiz and revealed its results. The people who seemed especially disappointed were those who assumed Michael would be in the same house as them: somehow an online quiz based on a fictional world had put a line between them that hadn't been there before.*

---

* Of course, we were still all united by the shared social identity of being 'people who debate Hogwarts houses over dinner', so this wasn't too disastrous.

Here are two more examples of group stereotypes:

1. Michael is an economist. As a result, you might predict that he's going to be mathematically minded, attached to theoretical models of human behaviour and also possibly a bit arrogant.
2. Susannah is vegetarian. As a result you might predict that she is going to be more difficult to cater for at dinner parties, is going to talk constantly about being vegetarian and make you feel bad about eating meat, and also be slightly smug.

These are stereotypes of particular social identity groups to which we actually do belong, and do resemble many economists or vegetarians.

Of course, in reality, these stereotypes don't perfectly explain the behaviour of all members of the group. Michael is, in fact, much more interested in applied rather than theoretical economics, and Susannah often reminisces about how delicious bacon is. However, when we operate in a realm where a particular social identity is salient, we are conscious of these stereotypes and whether we are adhering to or violating them.*

When Michael goes to economics conferences, he ends up talking a great deal about constrained optimization and identification strategies. When Susannah goes out to dinner with other vegetarians, at some point the conversation turns to the topic of cheese – how delicious it is, what a pity it is that many cheeses aren't actually vegetarian, and the question of where the

---

* Susannah, for example, is conscious of how much of this chapter has involved references to vegetarianism or veganism …

moral line is between eating meat and consuming dairy products. This conversation is, of course, pretty dull for any omnivores in the group (while the vegans are biting their tongues to keep from interjecting), but it's just one of those things that happens when two or more vegetarians sit down to eat.

The groups we're part of influence our behaviour in more than just conversation. Although this strand of research is in its infancy, there's some evidence already emerging that shows us that communicating to people that particular behaviours are consistent with their established social groups – or groups they might want to be included in – can encourage healthy eating in adolescents,[47] reduce propensity to cheat[48] and increase children's willingness to help others.[49]

As we've seen already, we can have lots of group identities floating around in our head at the same time. An interesting and important question therefore is how people come to identify more or less strongly with particular groups. We talked about this a little when we looked at identity threat: the combination of a threat to the group and a weakly held identity can lead to someone's group identification being further reduced – or even to them exiting the group altogether. People do this all the time, by changing jobs, changing groups of friends or changing the way they think about themselves. If Michael started to wish he got mocked less about using quite so many *Star Trek* references,* he could stop acting consistently with the social group of Trekkie.

Our ball-toss players from Chapter 2 may have found rejection by their two Klansman co-players painful, but for most of them it probably faded from mind pretty quickly – 'computerized Klansmen

---

* By Susannah.

I am playing a ball-toss game with in a lab' was presumably not a deeply held social group. Other social categories, though, are stable and fundamental parts of how we see ourselves and others, form patterns of behaviour and understand the world. Identity threats against this kind of social group can lead to a deepening of someone's ties to the group, like the Trump-supporting deplorables we saw in Chapter 2.

Early research proposed that the strength of any group identification was mainly about esteem: that people would identify more with groups that made them feel good about themselves. But that docsn't explain the puzzle of why people would continue to identify with groups that didn't: why the Deplorables doubled down on 'Make America Great Again'; why people from disadvantaged communities do not just reject those communities and assimilate into dominant majorities; or why die-hard fans of the England cricket team became even more committed during a thirty-year drought of winning the Ashes.

In fact, what we seek is something called *optimal distinctiveness*, where our level of identification with particular social identities depends on how well they balance our need for belongingness and validation with our need for distinctiveness and individuality. We find the former within the group, while the latter is satisfied by comparing ourselves with other groups. The implication of this is that our most strongly held social identities will be those where the group is close and homogeneous enough that it gives us a clear sense of who group members are and what group membership means, but also allows us to distinguish ourselves from others outside the group. Essentially, we don't so much want to stand out from the crowd as we want our crowd to stand out from other crowds.

Another hint about what causes us to identify more or less strongly with particular identities lies in the work the Behavioural Insights Team did with King's College London to understand the experiences of first-year students at King's. Susannah, working with Lucy Makinson from BIT and Anne-Marie Canning and Maija Koponen from King's, recruited 750 students into a six-wave survey, asking them at set points over the year how they were feeling and what they were doing. One of the things asked in the fourth wave of the survey – about two thirds of the way through the year – was for the students to rank how much they identified with various aspects of the university. The three most highly ranked were 'my course', 'my campus' and 'all of King's College London'. Many students also identified with a student society (more on this in Chapter 11), but fewer than half ranked their faculty or department in the top three.

This makes sense. Your course mates, with whom you share classes, tutors and exam schedules, can give you a sense of belonging and affiliation – and, as we've noted above, some of our most powerful social identities are attached to small, interactive groups. Meanwhile, interacting with students on other courses gives you the opportunity to think about how your course is different, and superior, to others.

King's is organized around multiple campuses, which are scattered across London. Students will be based at one campus but their classes and activities may take them to others. The campuses all have distinct characters, from the medical facilities at Guy's and St Thomas's and Denmark Hill, to Somerset House, which is part of the Strand Campus. Campuses are the frameworks within which students experience university, and give them cues about who they are and how they fit in (we explore this further in Chapter 7). Going to other campuses gives students further opportunity to think about how they are different, and to prefer the familiar halls and walkways of their own campus.

In the survey, we also found that low-income students were significantly more likely to list the whole of King's College London as their top identification. Perhaps these students felt more acutely the symbolic value of the institution, and what it meant to them to be at a top-ranked university in comparison to their friends from school. It's also possible that these students were less likely to have built strong interpersonal relationships with their course mates (more on this in Chapter 11).

We also wanted to encourage first years to sign up to King's Connect, the King's alumni mentoring platform. Building on this identity insight, we explored whether students would be more likely to sign up for mentoring if they perceived a shared identity between themselves and the mentor. Accordingly, we had designed two sets of text messages (alongside a non-texted control), one of which focused on informational content while the other added an element of shared identity as King's student and King's alumnus.

> Hi Aisha, as a first-year student you'll have lots of questions and decisions to make about your studies over the next few years. It can be great to ask someone who's been in your shoes and has ended up where you want to be. Did you know all the alumni on King's Connect have signed up just so that you can get in touch with them? They want to help you get the most out of your time at King's. Sign up here: #link

Overall, more students signed up to King's Connect in the identity condition. But most strikingly, *no* low-income students signed up in the control or the factual condition but in the identity condition *more* low-income students signed up than any other group. It seems that those students needed the push of the shared identity to encourage them to reach out.

It is perhaps obvious from the above that a powerful form of social identity is connected with the world of work – the way we identify ourselves based on our role in a company, as part of the team that we sit in and in the company as a whole. The workplace provides a series of cascading identity groups, forming perceptions of the 'typical' worker and leading us to make comparisons with other groups. People may have a social identity connected to their whole organization, to their branch or site, to their work group, their discipline and their rank, and these overlap and interact with each other over the course of a working day. This is why a common cause (or a common rival, like another sales team in the organization, or an opposing sports team) is so important to organizational cohesion: without relatively frequent signals that members of the organization should be focusing their comparisons (and their quest for positive differentiation) on an external group, the likelihood is that they will, instead, focus on positively differentiating themselves from groups who are closer to hand, be that forming a rivalry with HR or looking down on members of the regional offices.

Another thing that came up in Chapter 1 was the increasing congruence of political identities: how the gradual alignment of the Republican Party with white, Christian, working-class voters created increasing intolerance of other groups. One survey found that respondents who saw their various social groups as similar or even overlapping would be more likely to punish other people for violating the group's norms, and to discriminate against other groups.[50] No surprises here: the greater the extent to which we can act consistently with the ideals of most of our social groups at once, the more we are going to feel like we belong within those groups, and the more deeply we will identify with them.

But what can be done about the increasing divisions in society, and more generally within groups? Can social identity theory, developed to understand why groups get into conflict with each other, also be used to understand how groups can live in harmony?

Conflict between groups has been a feature of human society for as long as humans have been social, but social identity theory is a relatively young field that is still developing. Although there is a great deal of research from within and beyond social psychology into prejudice and its remedies, very few of these studies are of high empirical quality. There is undoubtedly a long way to go on understanding how we can mobilize people's identities towards positive change.

This might all seem quite abstract, and perhaps a matter for governments to deal with, but we're all part of the social fabric of society. The way we conceptualize the groups we belong to influences the behaviour of others in the group, and the way we interact with those who are outside our groups can have a profound impact on them – especially if we're part of a privileged majority. These small interactions between people, and between groups, aggregate up into political systems, polarization, intolerance and even potentially violence between groups. It's important that we look at ourselves and think about the ways that our own group membership influences the way we think and act, and the way that we see others.

And if we see intolerance in others, we can tell them we don't think it's OK – especially if they're part of our social groups. We are starting to see some evidence that framing a thought or idea in terms of a social group that people value can be used to encourage us to behave in a way we think is consistent with the ideal of that social group. Fans of George R. R. Martin's *Game of Thrones* will be familiar with the motto 'A Lannister always pays his debts'. A powerful statement of the 'ideal' of a social group (in this case, a family) that the Lannisters live up to with gruesome consequences. Imagine that instead of that we could say, 'Being American means listening carefully to those we disagree with' or 'We don't do that at this school'.[51]

Studies have shown that people whose various social groups provide some conflict in prescribed behaviour – like being a New Yorker who supports the Boston Red Sox – are less likely to be hostile toward other groups.[52] Although it's not clear whether this is because those of us who are more open to complexity are also more open-minded or because complexity leads to open-mindedness, this finding could be a potential pathway towards devising ways of increasing tolerance between social groups. It is clear that we should resist the temptation to think about complex matters such as identity in simple terms: ours or others. Think about a time you've felt like you acted against what others expected of you, or when you felt trapped because your friends expected one thing of you and your work another, or when you felt like you were acting inconsistently with how you were supposed to due to your gender, ethnicity, sexuality or age. Hold on to that feeling, that complexity, and remember when you interact with others that they are probably also navigating a web of different social groups and expectations.

There is also research that suggests that contact with members of other groups can be valuable. To the extent that people's group identifications are becoming deep and harmonious, they are more likely to interact with people from those groups and less likely to encounter people from other groups. How often do you interact on an interpersonal level (i.e., not in passing, in a shop, or as casual chit-chat) with someone from a very different social background to you? If you think about it, the answer may be 'Less than I thought'. If you're a lawyer, the chances are that most of your friends are lawyers. If you're British (and live outside London), chances are that most of your friends are British. If you're middle class, you probably mostly hang around with middle-class people. And if you're a middle-class British lawyer, odds are that most of your friends are at least two of those things as well. Social media has made this problem more severe, with people being able to separate themselves off into a 'Facebook bubble' and never encounter people with opposing social groups or views. Meeting someone from another group means interacting with them on an interpersonal level, reducing social distance (which we discuss in the next chapter); but it may also serve to reduce the extent of negative stereotyping.

There is some interesting research that suggests that certain psychological exercises can reduce our tendency to distance ourselves from those outside our social groups. For instance, encouraging people to interact as individuals by getting them to focus on things that are not related to social-group membership, particularly each other's unique individual characteristics.

This doesn't tend to happen, though, especially in Britain where the norm is to keep conversation light and 'small': with approved topics such as 'How was your weekend?' and 'Good/bad weather we're having, aren't we?'

But changing these conversations from the superficial to the interpersonal isn't difficult. There's a protocol called the

Experimental Generation of Interpersonal Closeness,[53] which is a set of thirty-six questions that aim to generate the kind of feeling of closeness between people that usually arises from years of friendship (this is useful to psychological researchers who wish to study the behaviour of people with close bonds). The first question on the list is, 'Given the choice of anyone in the world, who would you want as a dinner guest?' and the questions escalate in intimacy until the thirty-sixth question, which asks you to share a personal problem and seek advice on how to solve it.

How often do you ask a new colleague or acquaintance a question like, 'What would constitute a "perfect" day for you?' or 'What in your life are you most grateful for?' Meaningful conversations like these are the fast-track to interpersonal connections that span social groups.

Another way to overcome prejudice is to encourage people to identify with an overarching social group to which they all belong, moving their focus away from their more immediate group. (As we talked about in Chapter 1, after an election, politicians may try to encourage Democrat voters and Republican voters to focus on the shared social group of 'American'.) We can also encourage people to find a social group they have in common; for example, identifying shared interests or values – like a sports team they both support, or a shared love of Taiwanese food. Studies suggest that all these approaches have the potential to reduce prejudice against members of other social groups.[54]

Perspective-taking, where people are encouraged to sit down and think about an issue from the other person's point of view, is also an interesting way of reducing negative stereotyping of others.

Imagine you've just been snapped at by someone in the New York office. You might think, 'All New Yorkers are rude; I won't involve them next time if they're going to react like that.' But if you sit down and think, 'What would it be like to be a member of the New York office? Why might this person have reacted the way they did?' you might realize that you scheduled the call for 6.30 p.m. New York time, and that the office is in the middle of Manhattan so maybe it's a long, stressful commute home for your colleague. You might remember that the person you spoke to has just taken on a lot of additional responsibility, or has struggled to be accepted in the New York office because they're from the Midwest and everyone else is from the East Coast. And then you might revise your initial uncharitable judgement of the character of the colleague who snapped at you.

Although perspective-taking may be able to bring about a change in attitude towards the individual whose perspective is being taken (your colleague), it doesn't seem to bring about an overall change in perceptions about the social group to which that individual belongs (you might keep thinking that New Yorkers are rude).[55]

However, although the types of approaches outlined above aim to increase contact and empathy with members of other groups, one of the main insights from social identity theory is that the most effective way to change attitudes or reduce prejudice may be to work from within the group, rather than increasing contact with those outside the group. But what does this mean in practice?

Our attitudes towards others, and the stereotypes we have about them, are formed by the information flowing within our own social group. We learn to expect that fans of the opposing sports team are rude, uncouth and unsporting by hearing stories about their behaviour by fellow fans of our own team. We learn that the marketing department are lazy from hearing colleagues complain about them – and, in turn, we collect our own stories about our run-ins with marketing and pass them on to our colleagues. As we've explored in this chapter, this is a natural part of groups: we want to differentiate ourselves from other groups and feel like we are more sporting or motivated or whatever than they are. However, if the norm or expectation within the group is that we assume the best of others, seek to take others' perspectives and seek out opposing viewpoints to our own, then this could be the most powerful way to reduce intergroup conflict. Along with reducing the perceived social distance between individuals from different backgrounds, positively influencing the norms, cues and information flowing within networks are the focus of social choice architecture.

In this chapter, we've looked at the formation of social groups; at the way group members are constantly engaged in a negotiation about what the 'ideal' member is like, and expect members of the group to resemble this stereotype. We've also explored what causes people to identify strongly with particular groups, and what kinds of groups are most likely to meet their need for 'optimal distinctiveness'.

Now that we've got an understanding of how information and expectations flow through groups, we can start to think about how to design teams, workplaces and policies, so that they get the best – not the worst – out of people's social natures.

5

Social Distance

'The only difference between man and man all the world over is one of degree, and not of kind, even as there is between trees of the same species.'

Mahatma Gandhi

I N ONE OF what has become an iconic set of studies taught to every undergraduate economist, psychologist Daniel Kahneman and behavioural economists Jack Knetsch and Richard Thaler brought students into the lab and got them to play a game. The game couldn't be simpler: one student was given an amount of money – let's say $10 – and asked how much money they'd like to give to the other player, who has received nothing.[56] The first student (the Decider) chose, and then they left with their $10 minus however much they'd given to the other student (the Receiver). This is what economists call a Dictator Game,* and will be familiar to anyone who has ever taken even the most basic game-theory class.

In the lab, students make their decisions in isolation – literally in separate booths – and don't know who they're giving to, or, if

---

* Sticklers (like Michael) will note that the Dictator Game isn't strictly speaking a game, which would require strategic interactions between two or more players. Susannah would add that it also doesn't fit the lay definition of a game, since games are supposed to be fun.

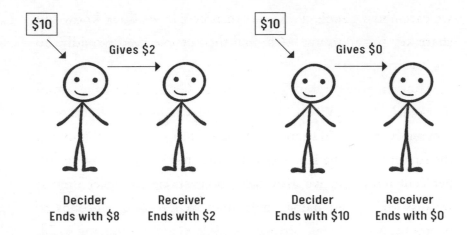

| Decider | Receiver | Decider | Receiver |
| Ends with $8 | Ends with $2 | Ends with $10 | Ends with $0 |

they're the Receiver, who is giving them the money (or not giving it to them, as the case may be). In this simple formulation, there's a clear best strategy for the Decider. Any amount of money given away makes the Decider worse off, so they should give as little as they can: nothing. A certain type of economist not only understands the concept at play here (a *dominant strategy equilibrium*) but also genuinely expects this to happen.

Of course, in reality, hardly anyone donates nothing, leading economists to accept (some of them more grudgingly than others) that people are not as callous and self-serving as their theories predict. Kahneman, Knetsch and Thaler were therefore able to conclude that people have *pro-social preferences* – or, as most people would say, people care about other people.[57]

But when, and how, and to what extent do people care about other people? If we can answer these questions, then we can design workplaces and other environments to maximize positive behaviours. In many ways this comes down to social distance: the perceived degree of separation between two people, based on their interpersonal and social-group relationships. First and foremost, we care about people we know; then people we don't know but share key social groups with; and then people more broadly. So far, so straightforward.

Another study reran this Dictator Game, with one small difference. They told Deciders the first name of the Receiver.[58] Obviously they could simply have made one up,[59] but just knowing the first name of the Receiver led people to donate on average 48 per cent more. So, we also care about specific people, even if we just know their name, more than we care about groups of people or just the vague concept of 'other people'. Reducing social distance between the two players, even in a purely cosmetic way, made people more generous.

Another example of this can be found in one of the reasons why American universities routinely raise substantially more than British universities in donations from alumni. Anyone who has experience of both systems can tell you that British universities seem disorganized and amateurish by comparison to their American counterparts, who seem to have the process of extracting donations from their alumni down to an exact science. This is partly because they really *do* have it down to an exact science. One of the practitioners of this science is Jonathan Meer, a professor at Texas A&M University, who has over the last ten years worked with several universities to try to understand the psychology of fundraising through alumni – and in doing so has contributed substantially to those institutions' coffers.

The case of getting someone to donate to their former university is an interesting one. The best evidence we have says that people benefit from going to university quite a lot in terms of their lifetime income – about £200,000 extra over the course of their life in the UK, or $1 million in the US.[60] Of course, some degrees are more lucrative than others, with economics, law and medicine regularly topping the charts, while some estimates show that a degree in art history actually *decreases* how much you can expect to earn. Regardless, most people seem to think that university is good for you, and something to be encouraged.

However, many people are reluctant to hand over money to their universities after they graduate. Part of this may be to do with tuition fees – people feel that they've already paid for their university experience once, and don't feel that they owe some kind of moral debt to the institution; after all, most of them will bear a very real financial debt for potentially decades after they graduate.

But the UK system of student-loan repayment, while considered horrific by many Brits, is extraordinarily gentle compared to the American system. Tuition fees are (at the time of writing) capped at £9,000 per year for a three-year course – the norm in the UK. Together with loans for living expenses, the average graduate in 2018 will have £50,700 in debt when they graduate.[61] Repayment doesn't begin until after a student graduates and is earning more than £21,000 a year – a higher salary than 46 per cent of workers earn in the UK.[62] Student loans are written off after thirty years, and the Institute of Fiscal Studies estimates that about three quarters of all students will never pay back their debts.[63]

Contrast this with the US. Fees vary substantially from university to university in America, as the whole system isn't so heavily regulated, but Harvard is a particularly salient example. Annual tuition fees at Harvard were $43,000[64] in 2017, rising to $63,000 with the inclusion of rent and board. At today's prices (and thanks in no small part to Brexit) that's £47,419 per year – not much less than a British student will accrue over their entire time at university – and payable for four years of study rather than the UK's three, without the protections provided by the British government.

Now, it's not for us to judge which of these systems is better, or whether a Harvard education is indeed worth about four times as much as one from Oxford, but it does raise the question of why Harvard students give so much back in donations. Despite paying far more in fees, and accumulating far more debt, Harvard alumni donated $1.2 billion (£900 million) in 2016, compared to the £345 million[65] ($458 million) raised by former students of Oxford.

Part of the general culture of American alumni fundraising is that as well as the usual letters and introductions to the alumni magazine asking for money, former students receive telephone calls from fundraisers asking for donations. This is a little invasive, but it is at least less intrusive than being accosted in the street or door-knocked.

Meer looked at data from one university's telephone fundraising campaigns, to examine the effect of social distance between the fundraiser and the alumni. He found that geographical distance – how close by the fundraiser and the donor lived to each other, or had done in the past – made no difference to how much the potential donors gave.

So what about the relevance of social groups – the connecting ties between the donor and the fundraiser? Being in the same fraternity or sorority as each other was worth about an extra 8 per cent donated, and having the same 'academic honors' status (getting the same type of degree) was worth another 9 per cent. Pretty substantial increases when you consider that the average amount given was $614.

Meer realized that the people making the fundraising calls weren't just undergraduate students toiling for minimum wage, as you might expect – instead, many of them were alumni themselves. In some cases, they had once been the roommates of the people they were calling. Imagine being called up not by a total stranger, but by someone you had spent a year living in the same room with. Either you'd hang up immediately (that kind of experience is bound to leave some scars), or maybe you'd stop and listen to what they have to say. You might even find it a bit more difficult to say no when they ask you to donate some money to help, say, build the new science centre at the university. In fact, that's exactly what happens: people are 5 per cent more likely to give if they're asked to by their old roommate than by a stranger, and if they do donate, they give 17.5 per cent more. In the end, this strategy nets 25 per cent more money than having people called by someone else.

Of course, in the real world it can be pretty difficult to make sure that all of your customers are talking to someone they know well when they're thinking about buying a product or donating. Deborah Small, a professor at the University of Pennsylvania, worked with colleagues to change marketing materials for a fundraising campaign – this time using letters and fliers rather than a phone call.[66]

People were shown a campaign for Save the Children, focused on helping alleviate famine in Southern Africa and Ethiopia. The people in the study were split into two groups. The first group got statistical information detailing the size and scale of the crisis, and how many people were affected by it, based on information provided by Save the Children, which included statements such as '3 million Zambians face hunger', and '11 million people in

Ethiopia need immediate food assistance'. The other group were shown a picture of a little girl, and given specific information about her – saying 'any money that you donate will go to Rokia, a seven-year-old girl from Mali, Africa. Rokia is desperately poor and faces a threat of extreme hunger or even starvation. Her life will be 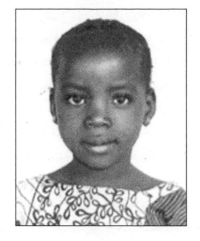 changed for the better as a result of your financial gift.'

Rationally, we know that the first set of information should be more important in guiding our decisions. As Spock[67] said, 'The needs of the many outweigh the needs of the few, or the one' – surely we should be more likely to donate to help millions of people than we are to help one person? However, perhaps unsurprisingly, this isn't the case. In fact, people donate on average twice as much when they're shown a single identifiable victim compared to when they're given the statistics.

The more we know about the one person, and the closer we're made to feel to them, the more we give. In a similar study, researchers at the Hebrew University in Jerusalem gave prospective donors information about sick children in an Israeli medical centre. Some people were given no information about the children, while others were told a child or children's age, or their age and their name, or were given their name and their age and a picture of them. The study found that the more information people had about the child, the more they were likely to donate, this time quadrupling how likely there were to donate between the messages that had the largest social distance and the smallest.[68] Interestingly, the same study found that there seems to be something particularly special about a single, identifiable person. People who received information asking them to help eight named children did not vary their donation at all depending on the level of social information that was provided about them. One may be the loneliest number, but it seems to be the best for getting people to care.

For people who care about charity effectiveness, this can often be dispiriting. The idea that the best marketing (rather than how much good a charity can do or the severity of the problem it is tackling) determines where the most money goes should give us pause – if our social instincts are outweighing our rational brain here, perhaps they're steering us down the wrong path.

That's what Deborah Small thought. She (and others since) has tried to help us overcome our basic social instincts, to make us more effective donors. In the same Rokia study discussed earlier in this chapter, some people were given an advance warning that they might be biased:

> *We'd like to tell you about some research conducted by social scientists. This research shows that people typically react more strongly to specific people who have problems than to statistics about people with problems.*[69]

The idea here is simple – by letting people know that they're biased towards identifiable, singular victims, we can maybe help them think twice, and make bigger donations when they see evidence, or at least be less swayed by the picture of Rokia.

So, did it work? Sort of. Telling people that they might be influenced by the picture of Rokia and her story decreased the extent to which people who saw it donated more than people who just got the statistics – but the same types of warning didn't increase the *amount* that people donated when they were given the information. It seems like we can suppress our social instincts temporarily if we're told that we should, but we can't make ourselves care about the dry figures – we're just *too* social.

Social distance also exists inside organizations – either between employees and their managers, or, commonly, between sales and marketing staff and their customers. One option is to narrow the social distance between the customer and the salesperson – similar to what we saw Jonathan Meer doing in university fundraising – perhaps by drawing attention to shared characteristics or experiences. Another option though is to work on the salesperson themselves.

That's what organizational psychologist Adam Grant did. One strand of Grant's work is concerned with *intrinsic motivation* – the things we do because we want to, not because of the pay attached to them. Sure, you work mainly for the money (certainly, if they didn't pay you, you'd need to find some other way to feed yourself), but when you go the extra mile for your colleagues, or your customers, or when you develop a new process that makes life easier for other people at the firm – that's intrinsic motivation at work. When you're doing something only because you're paid to, or because of some other form of reward (or hope of a reward), that's *extrinsic motivation*.

Extrinsic motivation might be reliable – if I pay you to do something, I've got a pretty good bet that you'll do it; whereas if I rely on you turning up to work every day out of the goodness of your heart, I'm probably on a hiding to nothing – but it's also expensive, and it only goes so far. Pay might get you to do your job, and performance-related pay might get you to do it better, but you can't pay people to go the extra mile, or to be team players.

Many organizations are dependent on intrinsic motivation. At the Behavioural Insights Team, Michael liked to welcome people to the team by saying, 'Welcome to T-REX* – the hours are long, but the pay *is* terrible.' The same can be said of most governments, charities and a large number of businesses that do something other than just make as much money as possible. Employees are willing to accept lower pay, for the feeling that they are helping their customers, or their teammates, or making the world a better place.

As Adam Grant found, this isn't just a given as a part of the job. Grant studied radiographers in hospitals – the people who administer and interpret tests such as X-rays and CT scans. These people play a vital role in diagnosing patients' illnesses and making sure they get the right treatment. However, Grant found that, after a few years on the job, radiographers lost some of their intrinsic motivation – they forgot about the links between what they were doing and helping people, at least in part, and started just going through the motions.

What Grant did next is a good example of boosting intrinsic motivation by reducing the social distance between professionals and the people they are serving. In his study, some of the radiographers were given not just a patient's scan (a photo of their *insides*) but also a photo of the *outside* of that person. This simple intervention improved diagnosis accuracy by 47 per cent – not because there was any information in the photos of the

---

* The team is Team Research, Evaluation and eXperimentation, and is commonly known as T-REX.

outsides of the patients (there wasn't), but because the people seemed more real.

In other research, Grant found larger effects – a 400 per cent increase – when he brought the beneficiaries of university scholarships in to meet people in a call centre that fundraises for those scholarships. These call centre employees weren't getting paid extra for these meetings, and the encounters were quite brief, but here (as with the radiographers given only minimal additional visual information) it showed that closing the social distance between the worker and the beneficiary can enhance intrinsic motivation.

Another example in the workplace comes from Ryan Buell, a professor at Harvard Business School. Ryan worked with a campus restaurant at Harvard to see if they could improve the quality of their food. But Ryan isn't a chef, or even particularly a foodie. He didn't look at the freshness of the ingredients, or even to market research to find out what the customers wanted or what the main competitors were. Ryan is a behavioural scientist, so he looked straight at the motivations of the chef.

Think about a restaurant – perhaps the last one you went to. You go in and get taken by a waiter to a table. You look at your menu, and eventually you decide that you want the duck à l'orange. You tell your waiter, and fifteen minutes later it arrives – you eat it and enjoy it, you pay and you leave.

There has been plenty for you to enjoy in this process – the environment, the friendliness and manner of the waiter, the company of your dining companion, and, of course, the food itself. Now spare a moment's thought for the chef. They're out the back of the restaurant. A slip of paper appears at the pass, asking for a duck à l'orange, or a steak, or a mushroom risotto.

They make the food, they place it on the pass, and a waiter spirits it away through the kitchen's swing doors. They probably like cooking (you'd hope so), and they maybe have friends among their colleagues, but they're completely isolated from an important part of their job: your experience of the food.

So Buell and two of his colleagues, Tami Kim and Chia-Jung Tsay, set out to close the social distance between the chefs and the customers.[70] They rigged up iPads in the kitchen and cameras outside in the restaurant, and set up a videoconference between the two, so that some of the time the chefs could see the people whose food they were cooking (but not interact in any other way) and sometimes they couldn't. They found that when the cameras were on and the chefs could see the diners before the meal was cooked, they worked harder, producing food faster, which was then rated by diners as tastier. You might wonder about the logical next step – what happens when you let the diners see the chefs as they work?

When Buell and his colleagues set up the experiment so the diners could see the chefs (but the chefs couldn't see the diners) they found that the food was appreciated more by the diners than when the chefs could see them, but this difference wasn't statistically significant. But when both parties could see each other, the diners thought their food was even better, and valued it more highly. The fact that chefs work harder, and make better food, when they can see the customers but the customers can't see them suggests that this is more about an increase in their motivation to do their job well when they feel closer to the customer than it is to do with monitoring.

If social distance matters between customers and workers, what about between colleagues? Some companies put a lot of effort into lowering social barriers between employees to make sure that they can relate to each other and keep their intrinsic motivation for helping each other out high. Ice-breaking sessions and trust games are obvious, highly structured forms of this, but others, like 'Friday Fun Drinks', or the seemingly identical T-shirts worn by members of each team at Google, break down social distance in other ways.

Removing these barriers to motivation and co-operation is no doubt helpful in creating a smoothly functioning team, but, as we've seen already, too much active engagement of our social instincts can actually lead us to be less effective and make worse decisions.

In corporate life, the evidence suggests that more diverse teams perform better, even if we forego some of the benefits from social closeness. In the US, firms that had female representation at top managerial levels on average grew more and were more resilient – increasing their average value by \$42 million (£32 million[71]) – and this difference was even larger for firms whose business was particularly focused on research and development.[72]

The same is true of racial diversity. Looking at a large sample of US banks, researchers have found that banks that are racially diverse substantially outperform those that are more homogeneous. It's even true of political diversity: having a mix of Democrats and Republicans in a team, or right- and left-wingers – makes the team more effective; bipartisanship leads to genuinely better governance, as well as being popular with voters sick of ideological battles. But this diversity can be hard to achieve.

Speaking at the Behavioural Exchange conference at Harvard in 2016,[73] Katherine Phillips,[74] a professor at Columbia Business School, described her experience researching task performance in diverse and homogeneous groups. Across hundreds of such tasks, she said, 'the percentage of groups that [reach the right answer] is always higher in diverse groups than in homogeneous groups'. But what makes her research distinctive is that she investigates how people feel about this – what the people within the teams believed about the experience. Surprisingly, 'the homogeneous groups felt that they were more effective, and they're more confident in the decisions that they've made – even when they're wrong'. People in socially distant groups, expecting to have disagreement with their colleagues, work harder, prepare more and are more creative than people who can rely on a cosy consensus. Naturally, then, people are also less likely to choose to be in a diverse group – one with more social distance in it – because it's harder work, more conflictual.

In the workplace, and in our everyday lives, we are wired to respond more to people who are socially close to ourselves; and organizations that can shrink social distance between their staff and their customers, or between their donors and their beneficiaries, can potentially reap the benefits by increasing people's intrinsic desire to work, serve or buy. Inside the organization, we might see that social distance reduction makes our lives easier as managers and makes our team more willing to help each other out. This is great in those times when we need everyone to pull together to get something done.

The smoothness that we gain by reducing social distance comes at a cost, though. There are fewer ideas and innovations in teams with low social distance. This is because the lack of social distance also means there's a lack of variety – everyone has similar experiences, and probably thinks in much the same way. Some disagreement is unavoidable in situations with higher social distance, but there are clear benefits that come with it. Giving ourselves an easy life as leaders is actually wasting money.

So, is there a way to have the best of both worlds – to create trust within a diverse group? Perhaps the answer is rituals. Michael Norton and Francesca Gino, two professors at Harvard Business School, found that tearing up a photo of our ex can help us get over them faster, and that performing a ritual around food* enhances our enjoyment of consuming it. Norton thinks that such rituals could enhance productivity at work by creating a shared identity and goals – even if they start off very different. For instance, in the film *Legally Blonde: Red, White and Blonde*, Reese Witherspoon's character attempts to introduce a ritual in the office in the form of a 'Snap Cup', where staff put compliments about their colleagues

---

* For British readers, think using a fingernail to break the tinfoil wrapping in a KitKat and then snapping the chocolate fingers apart.

into the cup to be read out at the next team gathering. At the beginning of the movie this goes incredibly badly, but by the end, as the team has bonded and come to respect one another, the Snap Cup becomes a symbol of team cohesion.

Taking this further, the economist David Reinstein at the University of Exeter, England, wondered whether rituals could have a bigger purpose – showing us how trusting to be. Reinstein is interested in the problem not of who to trust, but of how much to trust in general – something that is likely to be important in a large organization with diverse teams. Asking people whether they can be trusted isn't likely to be that reliable. After all, talk is cheap;[75] and anyway, asking everyone individually whether they can be trusted could prove very time consuming. Instead, Reinstein proposes 'anonymous rituals' in which everyone in the company is encouraged to do something like a Christmas Secret Santa,[76] or contributing to a colleague's wedding present. The stakes are low, and as the process is anonymous there's no real chance of any individual being ostracized for failing to take part; so people will tend to either play by the rules and buy a present, or not buy a present but take one anyway, thus revealing how trustworthy they are. You can't tell who did what, but the number of people without presents will indicate how trustworthy the participants in general – which in turn tells people in the organization how trusting they should be. Such rituals can help us to overcome social distance by making it clear that distance may not actually affect how trustworthy someone is.

Reinstein's research is mainly concerned with fixing the low trust caused by social distance by giving us a more realistic impression of how much people outside our immediate group can be trusted. Could we take the opposite approach, and try to build trust by reducing perceived social distance? This is what we did in an experiment we ran in 2015 with young people taking part in the National Citizens' Service. At the start of their NCS programme, teenagers are assigned to groups that they'll spend time with, Robbers Cave style, for its duration. Because these groups are deliberately diverse – rich and poor, black and white – social distance often starts pretty high.

In our study, we got four groups to take part in ten-minute ice-breaking tasks when they first met. In the control group, it was business as usual: they were told to simply talk among themselves. Each of the three treatment groups were asked to talk respectively about their similarities, their differences or their strengths and weaknesses. The groups who talked about their similarities had significantly higher levels of trust four weeks later than the other groups – and performed marginally better in group tasks. Just talking about how you're similar to someone else reduces the perceived social distance between the two of you, and means you trust them more and work better with them.

In this chapter we've looked at how we respond to individuals when we feel like we're socially close – or not so close – to them. This social distance makes a difference not only to how we interact with other people, but also to whether we choose to interact with them at all (something that we'll return to in Chapter 11).

Social choice architecture helps to bring people together and reduce the social distance between them; without it our organizations are less enjoyable places to work, and it can be harder to recruit and retain the best people – and to deploy them effectively.

How are people inducted when they join your organization, or when they move teams within it? Is the induction procedure focused on reducing social distance – highlighting the similarities

– or just on getting people through the door and aware of the company's rules and procedures?

During your recruitment process are you doing everything you can to make the company seem amazing, exciting and aspirational? If you are, you're probably doing a good job of attracting people who feel comfortable in that kind of environment, but you may be missing out on star performers who've had a slightly different journey and find your glittering corridors to be socially remote. By trying to make your company more approachable, and narrowing that social distance – showing the range of people who work with you, or being open about the areas you're trying to improve – you can scoop up those candidates too.

Social distance is also a factor when people are moving within a company, and especially when they're moving between offices and even countries. KPMG (one of the 'big four' professional-services firms) has more than 4,500 staff devoted to 'global mobility', helping to move their clients' staff around the world and integrate into new countries. Historically this practice has revolved around helping people secure visas and accommodation and ensuring paperwork is in order so they can move seamlessly into work, but there's increasing awareness that a smooth transition can be prevented by the social distance between the person moving and their new environment and colleagues.

A big focus when assisting a person's move to a new company or team is helping them to understand the culture of the new place – whether that's the way that people introduce themselves at the beginning of meetings, or the after-work social scene, or even just that most of the team are part of the office yoga club. Thankfully, one of our social instincts is geared towards picking up on exactly this kind of thing: our responsiveness to social norms.

6

Social Norms

'There go the people. I must follow them, for I am their leader.'

Attributed to Alexandre Auguste Ledru-Rollin

T IS CLEAR that social groups, whether they are national, religious, cultural, familial or other, impact all of us through our desire to behave in a way that is consistent with other people in our social group. In this chapter, we're going to look at norms – the ways in which we learn and respond to the 'typical' or common behaviours of other people. Social norms are among the most powerful – and the subtlest – forms of social influence. We don't always feel the pull towards doing what the crowd is doing, but most of us move with it anyway. We follow the norm unconsciously, which makes it hard to stop ourselves from doing it, and therefore easier for people to use the norms of our social groups to manipulate us – for good and for ill.

Imagine you find yourself in a new town. Perhaps you're there for a conference. You've never been there before and you don't know anyone. Where do you go for dinner? If your hotel doesn't have a restaurant, there's no easy default option to go with. You wander into the main square close by and look around. From the centre of the square you can see two restaurants – they're both Italian restaurants and you like Italian food. Neither of them is a chain, and both serve a good selection of dishes that you like, at reasonable prices. You're hungry, and you need to decide between the two. What do you do?

If you're anything like us, you might have a quick look in the windows of both restaurants to see what they're like inside. But you're probably not looking at the décor. Instead, you're counting the people.

The first restaurant is empty, and the second has ten tables occupied – busy, but with plenty of space left. Unless you're actively reclusive, you probably choose the second restaurant.* It could be that you just like people, but it's also that you've learned something from the fact that this restaurant is busier: the presence of the other people suggests that this is the better of the two restaurants (especially given their similar menus and pricings).

You've also probably made this decision without giving it a lot of thought. You haven't weighed up the benefits and the costs, but rather made what most likely feels like a random snap decision. This type of decision-making, which makes use of what Daniel Kahneman calls 'fast', or System 1 thinking in his book *Thinking Fast and Slow*, is, evolutionarily, highly adaptive. Even when we don't know what we're doing, we (mostly) avoid the poisonous berries if we just eat the same ones as our fellow apes.

Conformity is interesting for a few reasons. Some of it is about learning (working out which berries are safe, where to cross a river, or which restaurants are good) while other aspects are about a desire to be part of the group, and perhaps even to avoid punishment (as we saw in Chapter 2, and which we'll revisit in the

---

* In fact, this is the case probably even if you're fairly reclusive. Michael (who, as most people will tell you, does not enjoy social situations) would certainly choose the busier restaurant, having dealt with the social awkwardness of being the solitary diner in a restaurant in Budapest *for a week*.

next chapter). As we discussed in Chapter 4, group membership is partly a process of understanding and negotiating the *meaning* of group membership, and prevailing norms provide information on the kinds of behaviours to which the group conforms.

Conformity to norms is often beneficial and most societies require it in some cases: obeying the law, respecting property rights and contribution to shared goods. Without this it is unlikely we could survive in villages, much less cities. The existence of agricultural economies, where farming replaced hunter-gathering, requires us to know that other people will follow a set of norms.

Even the most basic things that you do require social norms. Since the emergence of currency in Mesopotamia in 2000 BC – at that stage little more than a receipt for grain deposited in a warehouse – there has been a norm to act as though money has value. If that norm didn't exist, your neighbour wouldn't give you chickens in exchange for money; he'd need you to give him something useful, like some grain. Establishing a common value for grain and chicken would take time and if in its absence your neighbour wanted grain, he'd have to hope that you (or someone else who owns grain) were in the mood for chicken.

Economies without currencies are unstable and impose an enormous burden on trade, even where there are relatively few goods to be traded. The *Star Trek: Deep Space Nine* episode 'In the Cards'[77] offers a neat example of this. Here, Captain Sisko's son Jake and his friend Nog are trying to lift the captain's spirits by getting him a mint-condition 1951 Willie Mays baseball card.*

---

* For anyone who is sane or not American, baseball cards carry the picture of a baseball player in a given year, and are traded by enthusiasts as collectors' items.

They can't buy the card* and so embark in a series of trades with the senior staff (for example, improving the audio quality of Klingon Opera) to get hold of it. The episode is entertaining, but it would have been much simpler if they could just have purchased the card. Instead, they were left dependent on the 'coincidence of wants': your neighbour has to want what you've got at the same time that you want what they've got, in order for you both to trade.

Of course, we don't live in a utopian future with no currency, and so can pretty easily just trade using money, but the ability to do so is dependent on a shared delusion that money – be it metal, or paper, or plastic polymer, or numbers on a bank's database – is valuable, and that if your neighbour accepts some of it in exchange for his chickens, the next person he tries to buy something from will also accept it. It's a wonderful delusion because if everyone is deluded, then money *becomes* valuable and thus nobody is deluded.

If literally everything that we buy depends on social norms, it's not a surprise that societies are so keen to preserve them, and to weed out noncompliance. Compliance rituals, like going to church on a Sunday, allow us to see who in our community is following the rules and invested in the social norm – and who is not.

Conformity to norms appears to be hardwired into society, but it's also ingrained in our psychology, so that we're constantly subconsciously on the lookout for new norms to adhere to. Simon Gächter, a professor of the psychology of economic decisions at the University of Nottingham, conducted a novel experiment to

---

* The Federation, being either a post-capitalist utopia or a dystopian military junta, depending on your perspective, does not have a currency. *Deep Space Nine*, however, allows things to be bought from other races using gold-pressed latinum.

find out just how fast we conform to a new norm.[78] The basic premise of the experiment was simple, and one that had been run before. Groups of participants were formed at random and asked to contribute financially to a pot. Money contributed is multiplied and then divided among the group. Crucially, the amount that it's multiplied by is larger than 1 but smaller than the number of people in the group. Imagine the group size is five, then the multiplier might be four. For every pound you put in, four pounds is distributed to the group, so everyone – including you – gets 80p. The group is better off because of your contribution, but you are left 20p out of pocket. In this game, most groups find a level pretty quickly. At the beginning, some people will be very generous, others more miserly. In the next couple of rounds of the game, if there are lots of misers, the initially generous people reduce their donations; while if the misers are outnumbered, they tend to increase their own donations; and after a few rounds of the game most people are donating about the same amount.

Gächter's twist on this experiment was interesting. He asked participants to play the game in two groups at the same time, meaning that some people ended up simultaneously in one generous, high-contribution group (one with few misers) and in a low-contribution group (one with lots of misers). If they were just learning about the rules of the game, they should split the difference and contribute an average amount in both games. But that isn't what happened. In the first round, people behaved the same in both of their groups – essentially taking a guess at what the right thing to do might be – but very quickly started conforming to the norm of the group they were in. Even where punishment wasn't a possibility, we rapidly identify social norms and conform to them.

This has an obvious real-world parallel in different friendship groups. When Michael is with friends from home in the South West of England, he's partial to a rough cider,[79] but when he's with our hipster colleagues in London, he's much more likely to drink a small batch-craft American-style pale ale. Susannah, meanwhile, recently shocked her colleagues when she returned from a weekend wedding swearing like a sailor – most of the guests were fellow Australians.

Of course, not all norms are equal. Some norms build group cohesion and lead to positive action, while others can be damaging to us and our environment. A famous example of this came about when Arizona's Petrified Forest National Park wanted to prevent people from stealing their most prized commodity – the petrified forest itself. Visitors to the park, clearly enjoying the park's astonishing fossilized wood, would take it upon themselves to, well, take some upon themselves, and were stealing lumps of the petrified forest at an alarming rate. It takes only a few seconds to steal a piece of petrified forest, but it takes millions of years to make more.

Researchers worked with the park on how to quell this spate of thefts, putting up different signs in different locations in the park at different times of the day. Every two hours, the researchers would measure whether strategically located (and easy to steal) pieces of petrified wood had been stolen, and then change the signs over. Some of the signs made use of different social norms – 'Many past visitors have removed the petrified wood from the park, changing the natural state of the petrified forest' or 'The vast majority of past visitors have left the petrified wood in the park'. The former message was intended to show people that the forest was precious and at risk, but visitors seemed to take this to mean that stealing was the norm and were – following that norm – significantly more likely to steal for themselves, with results that damaged the environment permanently.

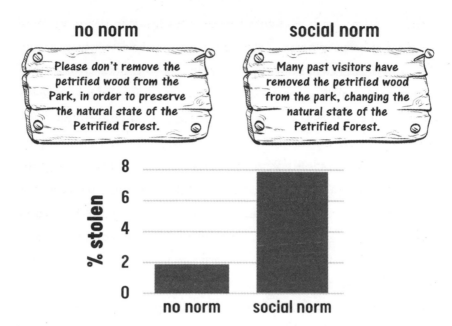

Results of the petrified wood social norms experiment, showing the proportion of pieces of wood stolen in different treatment conditions.

From this we can see that informing people that the undesirable norm was higher than they might expect (i.e., more people removed wood) backfired. But what about informing people that a desirable norm is lower than they might expect? One trial that attempted to answer this was carried out in an investment bank, where bankers who hadn't yet donated to charity as part of a nationwide fundraising campaign were asked to do so. Some were told that '7.5 per cent of employees in the UK have already given' – and staff reading this could see straight away that 92.5 per cent of employees *hadn't* given. As we might expect, including this line in the reminder email did not increase the likelihood of most employees giving. There were, however, some surprising effects on the most senior people in the bank – which we'll come back to later on.

Coming where it does in a chapter about how people conform to social norms, it might seem obvious that telling people the norm is low is a bad idea, but this is actually a common approach. For instance, pet shelters often struggle to get people to adopt black cats – whether this is because they are conventionally considered bad luck, or because they don't look good in selfies[80] – and many shelters have responded with campaigns that effectively say 'Nobody adopts black cats; isn't this shocking?' in an attempt to increase black cat adoption. Likewise, in the communal kitchen in one of our workplaces, where dirty dishes in the sink had collected on multiple occasions, a sign recently appeared featuring a photo of said dirty dishes, and asking us all to wash up promptly. These kinds of messages are common because the people who make them expect others to react the same way they do – with outrage and changed behaviour – but, rather like we saw in the petrified forest example, these messages may well backfire: people conform to the norm they've just been told about, rejecting the black cats at the shelter and abandoning their dishes in the sink for days ... just like everyone else.

If we're going to understand norms and their impacts, it's useful to know how they begin. Let's go back to the example from the beginning of the chapter – deciding on a restaurant in a strange town. You've made your choice and just sat down. Now, let's rewind forty-five minutes, to a time when both restaurants were completely empty. The first diner of the evening arrives in the square. Like you, she's from out of town – in fact, she's there for the same conference that you are – and doesn't have any information about which restaurant is better than the other. She goes through the same process as you: looks at the menus and prices, and tries to make the best decision that she can.

Arriving later, you have an obvious advantage over her, though: you can look to the crowd, but she can't; she has no one to follow. So, what does she do? She chooses a restaurant at random. It happens to be the second of the restaurants you looked at. Now, the next person turns up in the square – they have no better information than you did, or than the first person did, but they can now see her, sat in the restaurant at her table, not obviously dying of food poisoning, and so the best thing they can do, given the information they have, is to follow the first person to the same restaurant (unless they really *are* reclusive). Five minutes later, the third person arrives. They've now got slightly more information that leads them down the same path until, inevitably, you turn up and follow them as well. This is what's known as *herding*, which was first formalized by the economist Abhijit Banerjee in 1992.[81] Conforming to a social norm is just so natural that we follow scant evidence of one, even when we have no reason to believe that it's a good idea. In fact, you've ended up in a restaurant for no reason other than random chance – how good do you feel about your choice of restaurant now?

As you can imagine, this herding, conforming behaviour is also tempered by *who* we're conforming to. If the busy restaurant is a sports bar, filled with raucous fans of a rival team to our own, we may be less likely to join them than if it was filled with more nondescript professionals.

We've known for a long time about people's tendency to conform even when they know they're wrong. Solomon Asch's famous conformity experiment was, in fact, the first study Michael learned about in psychology back when he was sixteen. Asch found that even in a task with a clearly correct answer, most participants couldn't completely resist the temptation to conform to an incorrect consensus. Later work[82] shows that even participants who were familiar with the setup of the experiment, and the fact that the other players might have been lying, still conform to some extent to the group norm (although they conform less than uninformed participants).

This is interesting stuff, but is it *useful*? If people can be relied upon to conform to a social norm, doesn't it just happen naturally, without us thinking about it? If we want to influence people's behaviour, be it inside our organization, or that of our customers, or even as a government policymaker, is there a way to use norms for good?

The key to doing this lies partly in the fact that most of us often don't have a good sense of what the norm actually is: many behaviours that we might conform to are concealed, and this can lead us to over- or underestimate their prevalence. Think about the typical college environment. The perceived norm is that everyone is getting drunk every night, and that everyone is hooking up – these behaviours are highly salient, and in keeping with the stereotype of student life. However, they're actually not as common as we think and when students' beliefs are corrected, they tend to conform to the true, more sober, norm.[83] We saw the same thing back in Chapter 3 (page 46) with students overstating how socially connected and how popular other people are, potentially feeding their insatiable desire for social media just to keep up.

Very often, correcting these erroneous beliefs about the norm in a social group can have a soothing effect. In a study we ran at King's College London, students were sent a series of messages to try to encourage them to take up study-skills training offered by the college. Students, and new students in particular, are accustomed to finding studying if not easy then certainly manageable – otherwise they wouldn't have got into university. So the realization that they're struggling in their first year can come as a bit of a shock. Students can feel isolated and like they alone are failing. Ironically, this makes them less likely to take up training that could help them out, because they feel like they *shouldn't* need it, if all of their peers are doing just fine. Sure enough, when we texted students to say that 'Lots of King's first years find adapting to university study takes time', students were twice as likely to participate in the training.[84]

One of the first people to put the power of social norms to good use in government was Michael Hallsworth, now the managing director of BIT North America. Armed with insights from behavioural science research into social norms in the lab, Hallsworth conducted what was to be a seminal study. Working with John List, the University of Chicago Professor of Economics, Hallsworth worked to randomly change the letters that some taxpayers (or rather, non-taxpayers) received.[85] Looking at 100,000 people who were late in filing their 2010 tax returns, Hallsworth and his colleagues made subtle tweaks to the letters taxpayers were being sent. The body of the letters remained the same – a fairly dry reminder from the tax authority to file their returns and pay any owing taxes or face the (vaguely stipulated) consequences. But at the head of the letter, a single sentence was added. In the most basic formulation, this simply read:

Nine out of ten people pay their tax on time.

This message brought home that only a few people had not yet paid their taxes, making the social norm both clear (in case people hadn't been aware of it) and salient (in case people hadn't been considering it). This message alone increased the rate of people making a payment by 1 percentage point within the first twenty-eight days, compared to the letter without this message. In another version of the letter, Hallsworth made the norm specific, dialling up the sense of the reader being in a minority, with this message:

> Nine out of ten people in the UK pay their tax on time. You are currently in the very small minority of people who have not paid us yet.

This letter performed better still, increasing payment rates by another 2.4 percentage points compared to the first social-norm message, and 3.5 percentage points more than the letter without the social-norm message.

A second study went further again, introducing people's local area as a component of their identity, by comparing these two messages:

> The great majority of people in the UK pay their tax on time.

> The great majority of people in your local area pay their tax on time.

The addition of 'your local area' increased the impact of the social norm a little, but not statistically significantly. However, when this was paired with greater personalization of the messaging about *your* debt, the effect was larger, with just the addition of 'your local area' increasing payment rates by 2 percentage points.

> Most people with a debt like yours have paid it by now.

> The great majority of people in your local area pay their tax on time. Most people with a debt like yours have paid it by now.

These effects may sound modest, but taken together they contributed to bringing forward over £200 million ($270 million) in tax revenue each year.

The UK has a relatively high rate of tax compliance, but, fascinatingly, this same intervention worked in Guatemala, which has one of the lowest rates of tax compliance of any country in the world, so much so that they could only just say that 'most' people had already paid their taxes.[86] The important thing is that in Guatemala, even knowing that 'most' people paid their taxes changed recipients' perception of the social norm (which must have been that most people *didn't* pay their tax), and resulted in a change in behaviour of a similar magnitude in the UK.

Social norms are now some of the most widely used behavioural insights across the public sector globally, and what we've learned about them can hugely benefit organizations and individuals at very little cost.

This can be seen in Robert Cialdini's experiment with a local hotel chain. Cialdini, a professor at the University of Arizona, and colleagues[87] partnered with the chain to increase re-use of towels to save the hotel money and help protect the environment. They found that letting guests know that most people re-use their towels increased re-use by 34 per cent compared to a more moralistic message about the importance of the environment. On a larger scale, another study found that displaying households' energy consumption compared to their neighbours' on their statements either monthly or quarterly reduced their energy consumption compared to those households who didn't see the comparative information.[88]

Social norms can be used to encourage other behaviours in

consumers as well. For instance, solicitors in the Costa Rican National Park asking for donations changed the 'normal donation' they specified by saying:[89]

One of the most common donations has been [2/5/10] US dollars.

This short message gave people a sense of the prevailing social norm. Where before they had to make a decision about how much they thought was appropriate to donate, now their task was much easier because they'd been given a number to conform to. The researchers found that donations increased significantly the higher the reference point given.

Like most other things in life, social norms are not fixed. When our parents were growing up, smoking rates were far higher than they are now and many people would think nothing of driving their car after a few glasses of wine – something that would be unthinkable for most people today. This has two implications: first, the norms can be changed; and second, that as norms in our social groups change, we can adapt pretty quickly – meaning we can use social norms in organizations to help encourage behaviours that are not yet that common.

Online environments make it possible for researchers to see what happens when a norm changes. Online fundraising platforms are widely used in the UK to allow members of the public to raise money for a charity, very often related to them performing some feat of physical activity, or doing something dramatic (such as shaving their head[90] or legs*) or embarrassing (such as sitting in a bath of

---

* This particular activity is largely done by men in this context.

baked beans).[91] People's donations are recorded on the platform so that when a new person arrives they can see who donated before them and how much money they gave, as well as the running total and the target amount to be raised, if the fundraiser has set one.

Sarah Smith and colleagues from the University of Bristol analysed data from online donations made to people running in the 2010 London Marathon through two of these online fundraising platforms, JustGiving and Virgin Money Giving. By looking at the donations made before and after particularly large (or particularly small) donations, they were able to look at what happened to people's donations as the norm changed from donating small amounts to donating large amounts. The change was both instant – starting from the very next donations – and fairly large. A prominent £10 donation shifted the next few donations upwards by £2.50, with lasting effects on the 'normal' behaviour for donors. On the other side, particularly small donations also resulted in a small decline in donation levels, but this shift was less dramatic. The social norm here worked to set a minimum standard for behaviour, but it seemed to be what economists would call 'sticky downwards' – it's easier for us to adjust our norm up than it is to adjust it down, perhaps because we fear punishment for poor behaviour.

This kind of herding could be used in any kind of sequential marketing campaign, such as those for crowdfunding sites like Kickstarter. Website designers could make large donations, or rapid sequences, particularly obvious – for example by leaving the largest or top five pledges so far at the top of the page to make the norm clear. If pages have lots of very small pledges, which will decrease the average donation, displaying the median, which might be a better representation of the norm, might help to increase contributions. Websites like Amazon tell us what other people like us buy, and we follow the herd – Michael's kitchen has an overpriced silicone trivet as proof.

Let's also look at changes *within* organizations – can managers make use of social norms? The impact from within became clear through a project Michael worked on with the Movember Foundation, alongside Karen Tindall and Alex Gyani from BIT's office in Sydney. Movember is to blame for men across the English-speaking world abandoning their common sense and growing moustaches in November each year to raise money and awareness of men's health issues. Since 2015, Movember have also diversified into trying to increase men's physical activity, working with businesses to help encourage employees to get moving more. One project involved working with Lendlease, a construction company headquartered in Sydney and with offices all over Australia.

Lendlease had already invested in their employees' physical activity by buying them all wearable Fitbit devices, which tracked the number of steps they took and other types of physical activity throughout the day. Unfortunately, the data from these trackers showed that, although there had been an initial spike in activity after they were issued, and people were taking part in a 'Fitbit Challenge' in which people competed as part of their work teams to be the most active, the number of steps people were taking declined fairly rapidly over the next month.

Perhaps none of us would be surprised by this. Most of us when we get a Fitbit or a similar device use it persistently and aggressively for the first few weeks or months, pacing around the kitchen while we're waiting for the kettle to boil to get our step count just that little bit higher. But then, as time goes on, we forget that we're wearing it, and maybe we even stop wearing it because we forgot to charge it one evening, and our behaviour reverts to normal. Or maybe our behaviour gets worse, if we've substituted more physical activity for another slice of cake.[92] This was the finding of a long-term study carried out at the University of Pittsburgh, in which participants, all of whom were enrolled in a long-term behaviour-change programme, were divided into two groups – one with wearable devices and one without – and their activity was tracked over two years. At the end of the programme the study found that there was no difference between the two groups in terms of their levels of activity, and that the people who were given the wearables actually lost *less* weight than those who had just had the standard, technology-free programme.[93] A month after the initial challenge began at Lendlease, many of the staff were barely doing 1,000 steps a day. They were essentially sedentary. The intervention that we developed at BIT tried to turn the plastic wristband into a smarter tool for getting people active by leveraging their social connection to their colleagues. Working with Lendlease and Movember, groups of five were formed into mini-leagues, based on their prior performance in the October Fitbit Challenge, meaning that teams were competing against people that were similar to them in terms of performance. These groups have the hallmarks of strong social groups that can influence behaviour: they are small, interactive (being work teams), and have nearby comparison groups (in the form of other groups in the league) to try to out-compete.

Throughout November we sent everyone in the teams messages to let them know how they were getting on. As well as this, half the teams got social information about the norm within their group, and how far off they were from the leading group in their league. So they might have had a message like this:

＊fitbit

Lendlease Active Community sent you a
message:

"Team EH&S NSW, less than a week remains in the
MOVEmber Rematch - last day 30 November!

Your team is currently 2nd in your Challenge Group with an
average of 12,905 steps.

Make a final push for first place. Your team is only 1070 steps
per day behind Capella NSW, who is leading your Challenge
Group.

These messages went out every Tuesday morning, having been
calculated based on the past week's performance. At the end of
the trial, we compared the number of steps made by those who got
the social-comparison information to the number of steps taken
by people who just got information about their own performance.
The difference was bigger than we anticipated – an increase of
more than 600 steps (8 per cent) per day. The biggest effects were
concentrated on those people who had previously been the least
active: those who had been in the bottom quarter of the step count
increased their steps by almost 1,000 a day – nearly 50 per cent.
The combination of competition and the social norm of average
steps had a huge impact on their activity levels. But people who
were already very active, the top quarter, saw an increase of only
six steps per day. This isn't surprising, since they were above the
norm; if anything, we might expect their activity to go down. But
it's something that we need to be careful of when we're using social
norms in our own organizations: we're showing some people that
they need to work harder to meet the norm, but in doing so we

could also show those already exceeding the norm that it's ok to try less hard.

In 2015, Michael Hallsworth,[94] now working on health behaviours, teamed up with Professor Dame Sally Davies, Chief Medical Officer of England, to send letters to tell doctors who were heavily prescribing antibiotics that they were among the heaviest prescribers in their area and were hence deviating from the 'normal' level of prescribing. This letter, signed by Davies, reduced prescribing by these doctors by 3.3 per cent – and if this seems like a small amount, it was as much as the rest of the government's efforts to reduce antibiotic prescribing put together, but was much cheaper and easier to implement.

If we can nudge doctors to change their ingrained prescribing habits in this way, what else could social norms be used for? There are several examples of social norms applied to save lives. For example, by increasing organ donations and increasing attendance at hospital appointments by telling people that thousands of people like them sign up to be organ donors every day, or that nine out of ten people turn up to their appointments; and making it clear either that the behaviour is 'normal', or signalling that by not doing something you are standing out from the crowd.

Social norms can be a powerful force in the social environment, if used carefully. In general, social norms are particularly effective in bringing a minority in the social group into line with the desirable behaviour of the majority: getting high energy users to reduce consumption, getting tax-avoiders to pay their tax, getting college students to drink less, and so on. But we've seen important caveats to this: if the norm is lower than people expect, or the norm is actually a negative behaviour, then drawing attention to it can backfire.

We also need to think about how social norms fit into the rest of social choice architecture. In Chapters 4 and 5, we explored what makes people identify strongly with particular social groups, and to feel socially close to others. And it is clear that social norms will be more powerful in groups that people identify strongly with. In the Lendlease example, we provided participants with the average step count of competing small teams. We would expect that providing an average step count for the whole of Lendlease, or for everyone on the Fitbit app, would be less effective because it would feel less personal and less relevant. This example does also, however, highlight some pretty obvious limitations of social norms: what do we do in cases where the desired behaviour is not being practised by the majority? In this case, social norms are useless; we need to try to make that behaviour the norm, and that requires a different approach. In the next chapter we explore the other ways in which people can gain information about the normal (or desirable) behaviour among their social groups, and how these social cues form part of social choice architecture.

7

Social Cues

"'Cheshire Puss," she began, rather timidly, as she did not at all know whether it would like the name: however, it only grinned a little wider. "Come, it's pleased so far," thought Alice, and she went on. "Would you tell me, please, which way I ought to go from here?'"

Alice's Adventures in Wonderland, Lewis Carroll

SOCIAL CUES ARE clues in our environment that indicate what's expected of us, or what other people have got away with. They are closely related to social norms; in fact, in many ways they're a special case of norms.[95] But whereas before we focused on the explicit communication of norms (for example, telling people that nine out of ten taxpayers pay on time) or directly observed norms (like copying the restaurant choices of others), in this chapter we're looking at everything else that lets us know what's normal, what's commonplace and what's acceptable, in sometimes subtler and more pervasive ways. These cues include the ways that spaces are designed (telling us something about how the designers expect us to behave), the artefacts of people who have been there before us (telling us about how others have behaved) and our interactions with people (telling us how they expect us to behave).

Imagine it's a Monday morning and you're on your way to work. You walk out of your house and head towards the station, stopping in for a takeaway coffee. You finish your coffee just as you're getting on a train. It's crowded so you find a spot to stand, and someone bumps against your back, which you take to mean you should put your bag down on the ground. About halfway through your journey, you get a seat, moving aside several free newspapers. You put the empty coffee cup down at your feet, and when you get off the train you leave it there and head for your office.

You're a bit nervous – you've got your performance appraisal this morning, but you've had a pretty good year so you're also optimistic. Your boss calls you over, and you head into a meeting room and sit down. Your boss opens the conversation with, 'Now, it's nothing to worry about, but ...' and your heart sinks.

Already your day has been influenced by a series of cues all around you – the bump against your back, the newspapers on the seat, the foreboding opening sentence from your boss – which have changed the way you behave. Without really knowing it, we're constantly responding to social cues that shape our understanding about acceptable, normal behaviour. But cues can be even bigger than this – they can be built into physical spaces themselves.

The village of Poynton, near Manchester, England, had a problem. The community was in decline and village life was disintegrating because decades of traffic engineering had resulted in the heart of the village becoming an intersection of two arterial roads that was loud, dangerous for pedestrians and unappealing to visit.

So, in 2011, Poynton did something unusual: city planners removed all the traffic lights, reduced the approaches to the village centre from two lanes to one, and put up a series of visual cues to drivers that the highway had ended and they were entering a town.

The result, according to the people that live there, was a complete change in the way that road users interacted with each other: cars going more slowly and pausing for pedestrians, pedestrians waving to motorists as they crossed, and an increase in footfall to the local businesses – in short, the town came to feel more like a community.

Such 'shared space' schemes have their challenges,[96] but provide a fascinating insight into the ways in which the design of spaces can lead us towards certain models of behaviour. This isn't a new idea. In the fifteenth century, Italian architect Leon Battista Alberti argued that classical architecture could have a civilizing influence on invaders – so that barbarians at Rome's gates would naturally become less barbaric in the presence of the city's sights. Likewise, Poynton found that changing the cues in the physical environment had a civilizing influence on intercity traffic.

Susannah was so taken by the case of Poynton, in fact, that in her final interview for the Behavioural Insights Team, she enthusiastically pitched trying something similar on the busy Bank intersection in London. The interview panel requested that she propose something around education instead (which is fair, because the interview was for a role in BIT's education team).[97]

The point is, the social cues – and hence effects on our behaviour – in physical spaces can be profound. In the 1950s, Minoru Yamasaki, the architect who designed the World Trade Center, designed the social housing 'project' known as Pruitt-Igoe in St Louis, Missouri. Initially praised for its community-centred design, by the time the buildings were demolished in the 1970s Pruitt-Igoe was notorious for crime, squalor and social dysfunction. So, what went wrong?

A variety of things, by all accounts. The wide spaces between the buildings – intended to create space for communal activity – instead discouraged residents from developing a sense of community with those in other buildings, and visually separated Pruitt-Igoe from the surrounding neighbourhoods. Many of the stairwells served hundreds of families, making it impossible to tell resident from intruder. And the build quality, ventilation and maintenance were poor from the beginning, signalling to residents that they weren't valued.

British singer Tinie Tempah grew up on the Aylesbury Estate in South London, once described as one of the most notorious council estates in Britain, and has talked about it as a place that was 'designed for you not to succeed'. One of the most striking things about estates like this that we've seen during field work is the number of 'No Ball Games' signs in public spaces, sending a strong cue that even the open public space is not a place for fun or games, and potentially ceding it for more nefarious purposes.

Remember the petrified wood from the last chapter? In the same way that telling people about an unfavourable norm can sometimes shift their behaviour towards that norm, designers of social choice architecture (including designers of physical and digital architecture) may sometimes fail to recognize the cues they're creating or how they're being interpreted. In office buildings, dividers between desks might signal that this is an environment to work in isolation; while if the boss decides to sit with everyone else rather than having their own office, that gives a cue about how hierarchical the team is expected to be.

A growing body of research explores the impact of hot-desking on employees' identification with the organization, and is starting to find that hot-desking can undermine a sense of belongingness to the organization and reduce the strength of organizational units as social groups,[98] and create social hierarchies between employees who always use the same desk (and may be more senior) and those who have to move around.[99] It's almost certainly not the outcome employers intend when they implement hot-desking, but being allocated a permanent desk seems to send a social cue to employees that they have a place and permanency in the organization.

Cues in the environment, however, don't just come from the design of the buildings, interior spaces or streets. They come from how others have interacted with those buildings. Think back to your morning commute. You left your coffee cup on the floor of the train. Now, we don't know you; maybe you're the sort of person who regularly leaves litter behind you rather than carrying it until you find a bin … or maybe you were responding to a social cue you might not even have noticed.

When you sat down, you had to move a bunch of newspapers off your seat. This common experience of train commuters everywhere told you something about the people who commuted before you: it told you that they hadn't bothered to take their own litter off the train. Perhaps that was part of why you left your coffee cup behind?

A real-world example of this comes from Kees Keizer, a psychologist at the University of Groningen. Not content with studies showing that people conform to norms in the lab – and especially not just that trend-following students did so – he wanted to look at whether people take cues from their environment about what kinds of behaviour are socially acceptable: what they could get away with without judgement.

Keizer was inspired by the so-called 'broken windows' theory of crime prevention that became popular in the US in the 1990s, particularly under William Bratton, then head of the New York Transit Police. The theory went that the prevention of low-level crimes such as breaking windows creates an atmosphere of lawfulness and order, which in turn reduces the instances of more serious crimes like robbery and murder.

Keizer wanted to test this theory. Did disorder really spread through to other behaviours? He and his assistants set up a test. They fastidiously tidied an area of Amsterdam, in the Netherlands, to ensure that it was free of litter and graffiti, and then in turn deliberately messed it up, dropping litter and painting the walls with graffiti to create a disordered environment. With the area in both states – tidy and messed up – they stuck fliers advertising a (fake) sportswear shop to all of the bikes parked within it, using an elastic band to attach the flier to the handlebars in a way that necessitated the removal of the flier in order to ride the bike properly. There were no bins in the area so when people came to get their bikes at the end of each day, they had a choice: they could either drop the flier on the ground or take it with them. In the messy environment, two thirds of people littered – compared to only one third when the area was tidy and graffiti free.

What surrounds us in the physical world matters to how we interact with it. What about the virtual world? Every time we land on a website we are asked to agree to some form of data collection (usually, website cookies recording our visit), and when we sign up for a website, be it social media, online shopping or a news website, we agree to provide even more information.

Online privacy increasingly makes headline news, from the sale of personal data between companies, to the use of data from other websites to target ads elsewhere on the internet, to surveillance of private citizens by various government and non-government actors (some of which we discussed in Chapter 3) and so on. In 2018, a major breach at the online-survey website Typeform affected thousands of firms who use Typeform to collect data, including Monzo and Revolut, two 'challenger' banks set up since the financial crisis to disrupt the banks who caused the financial crisis, most of which were still in operation after the financial system was bailed out.

Although the breach was relatively modest, this was more a technical limitation than a practical one – the hackers got access to only a relatively small amount of Typeform's total stash of data. Everyone else who uses Typeform for data collection got lucky. Typeform's ubiquity as a data collection tool, and the ease with which we hand over our personal data – everything from names and addresses to salaries and other financial information – is startling only after the fact. As we tap in private information to our keyboard, we barely think about it.

But what makes us more or less willing to disclose our most personal information to corporations we interact with? Although one would hope it would be close reading of the privacy policy followed by careful consideration of the pros and cons of disclosure, it won't surprise readers of this book to know this isn't the case.

A series of studies has investigated how contextual cues make people more or less likely to disclose personal information and found that, paradoxically, people were nearly twice as willing[100] to share personal information (in this case, whether they'd engaged in sensitive behaviours such as cheating on a partner) on an unprofessional-looking website that had no mention of a privacy policy or data protection than they were on a more professional website.[101]

The researchers replicated this research on several different groups, including visitors to *The New York Times* website, and students, and found that in all cases people were more likely to disclose personal information on an unprofessional website than they were on a professional-looking one. Some examples of the websites they used are shown opposite – which seems safer to you?

The replication with students is particularly striking because the implied collector of the data was the university for both versions, meaning that students were more willing to disclose sensitive information to their university when it *wasn't* made clear to them that that data would be anonymized and treated responsibly.[102]

So why is this? It turns out that a professional-looking website and an obvious privacy policy send a cue to us that we should be worried about what is being done with our data, whereas some 'just-for-fun' site that would probably sell everything they know straight on to Cambridge Analytica ... just doesn't.

Our account of social cues so far has hopefully been interesting, but is strikingly incomplete: we haven't considered at all how our interactions with others within and outside our social groups shape our understanding of how we should behave. If these groups are important, then we'd expect them to influence the way we respond to social cues.

Let's start with the obvious: rewards and punishment. From around the time we start to develop independent reason, we're learning about the norms of behaviour our parents expect from us. Good behaviour is rewarded with approval – and sometimes ice cream – while bad behaviour lands us on the naughty step.

Over time, we get more sophisticated at assimilating cues from the environment around us into our way of approaching things.

Example 1

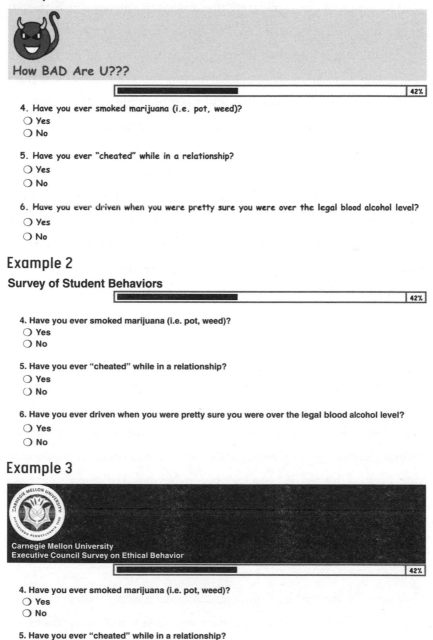

How BAD Are U???

|42%|

4. Have you ever smoked marijuana (i.e. pot, weed)?
○ Yes
○ No

5. Have you ever "cheated" while in a relationship?
○ Yes
○ No

6. Have you ever driven when you were pretty sure you were over the legal blood alcohol level?
○ Yes
○ No

Example 2

Survey of Student Behaviors

|42%|

4. Have you ever smoked marijuana (i.e. pot, weed)?
○ Yes
○ No

5. Have you ever "cheated" while in a relationship?
○ Yes
○ No

6. Have you ever driven when you were pretty sure you were over the legal blood alcohol level?
○ Yes
○ No

Example 3

Carnegie Mellon University
Executive Council Survey on Ethical Behavior

|42%|

4. Have you ever smoked marijuana (i.e. pot, weed)?
○ Yes
○ No

5. Have you ever "cheated" while in a relationship?
○ Yes
○ No

6. Have you ever driven when you were pretty sure you were over the legal blood alcohol level?
○ Yes
○ No

131

We learn that in the library we're expected to be quiet whereas in the cafeteria we can be louder; which patches of grass in the park can be walked on and which will earn us a stern word from the groundskeeper; and not to put our elbows on the table at a formal dinner even though we'd do it at home.[103]

We also get more inclined to convey our own expectations about the behaviour of others, whether it's 'accidentally' nudging the back of someone who hasn't put their bag on the floor of a crowded train, or sanctioning behaviour we disapprove of, such as greediness.

Our disapproval of greediness in others has been demonstrated in a series of lab experiments. One of us, let's say Susannah, is given an endowment of £10 and asked how much money she wants to offer to Michael. Susannah makes her offer, let's say, £4.* Michael can do nothing about it. This is a Dictator Game, which we wrote about in Chapter 5, where we saw that Deciders are more generous if they perceive lower social distance between them and the Receiver.

However, in this variation, a third party – that's you – can see the offer that Susannah has made. You've got your own pot of money, half the size of Susannah's (£5). If you don't like the offer that Susannah's made, you can choose to pay the researcher 50p – 10 per cent of your own money, to take £3 from Susannah. This money doesn't go to Michael – it just disappears back into the researcher's pot – but it sends a message to Susannah about what behaviour you think is acceptable.[104]

This experiment has been performed in fifteen very different communities on four continents and all the societies displayed the same tendency to punish when the offer was less fair, and to

---

* Susannah is, in this example, uncommonly generous.

be more likely to accept fairer offers. There was also substantial variation in this punishment behaviour between cultures, which seems to have been driven by differences in the altruism norm of those societies. In societies where altruistic behaviour is more prevalent, or considered of higher cultural importance, punishing selfish behaviour is more common.

Nobel laureate Elinor Ostrom studied the emergence of co-operation in laboratory games, and her work helps to shed light on how people start to co-operate in the real world. Although Ostrom's body of work is extensive and broad ranging, of particular interest for our purposes are the series of games that model collective-action problems: situations in which the interests of the group are served by all members contributing, but where each individual faces an incentive to 'free ride' or benefit from the contributions of others without contributing themselves. We see this in how we manage natural resources, for example. Everyone might be made individually better off by driving a gas-guzzling car that takes them from point A to point B faster than the bus, but if everyone does that we'll run out of petrol and global warming will make everyone worse off.

In the standard model of economic behaviour, all such problems play out in a similar way to the classic 'prisoner's dilemma' game. Everyone is better off if everyone contributes; but, because everyone is individually better off if they don't, people don't contribute. In the bleak world of economics, we never co-operate because there's nothing in it for us; and this creates what's known as the 'tragedy of the commons' – we all contribute too little to shared resources, and extract too much, meaning they're doomed to neglect and depletion.

Like much in the standard model of economics, though, this bleak picture doesn't survive contact with reality. Most common resources are contributed to, at least to some extent, and there are some real success stories.[105]

If economic agents are natural 'free-riders' who won't contribute unless the benefits to themselves outweigh the costs, then the world would perhaps be utopian if everyone was a 'co-operator', contributing regardless of the behaviour of others. The problem is that one free-rider can come along and exploit everyone else. Ostrom and her collaborators found that a great deal of successful co-operation in the real world rests with a third group – 'conditional co-operators' – who co-operate when others do, but reduce or cease their contributions if other people don't co-operate. Over time, free-riders learn from the responses of these conditional co-operators that free-riding will make them worse off; and that if they contribute, their own good act will crowd in others', allowing a norm of co-operation to emerge from the cues delivered by conditional co-operators.[106]

In the same way, members of social groups partly use cues to co-ordinate on what it means to be a member of that group. A classic example of this is the change in norms around smoking. Government has struggled to rapidly reduce smoking, despite overwhelming evidence that it's unbelievably stupid and harms not just yourself but those around you as well. Health warnings and taxes on smoking are successful to a point, but their effect has been slow relative to the size of the taxes and the proliferation of increasingly gruesome warnings.

A lot of the heavy lifting is also done by changes in social attitudes, which meant that smokers eventually found themselves on the receiving end of scrunched-up noses and pointed coughs signalling that their smoke wasn't welcome. In the UK, the smoking ban preventing people from smoking in pubs, restaurants, offices and other public places also sent a strong signal. Even though it wasn't enforced by the government, it allowed people to exile their smoking friends outside. We see the same kind of cultural change with seatbelt use and with drink driving. Although there are laws mandating seatbelt use, and banning smoking, these are largely unenforceable and the real drivers of our compliance are the reactions – real or anticipated – of our friends and family.

Although the role of our parents in communicating acceptable behaviour is largely superseded by the role of peers as we enter adolescence,[107] we continue to be sensitive to the cues we receive from people in positions of authority even if we see them as members of a different group to ourselves. In many ways, this underpins some of the cues that are embedded in architecture and design: at the other end of that design process there is a person, presumably authoritative, who has an expectation about how we're going to act. If an architect designed a staircase in a particular way, or made a corridor a particular height, we presume they did so for a reason and we accept that this is how the building works. When that design contains a social cue – for example a no-smoking sign in a bathroom – we figure that it was probably put there for a reason by someone who knew what they were doing. Or when a particular space makes us feel like we're not wanted or valued (think back to the 'No Ball Games' signs or the Pruitt-Igoe housing project) we may feel like there's a person in power on the other end of the design process who feels that way about us.

School teachers are often among the first authority figures we interact with outside the home. Five days a week for up to fourteen years, teachers provide us with a stream of social cues about how we're expected to behave, what we're expected to achieve and what our future prospects are. And these cues matter. Throughout adolescence, students are starting to develop a view of whether they can trust mainstream institutions and are becoming aware of negative stereotypes about their group.[108] One Canadian study found that by the time minority students reached high school, they were more likely than their majority peers to expect to be treated unfairly.[109]

A recent study compared teachers' expectations for children's grades to their actual grades and found that those students who were underestimated by teachers were less motivated, and perceived their teachers to be less accessible.[110] This is particularly prominent when we look at marginalized students, with the impact on achievement being between three and four times larger for these groups. Troublingly, research in the US also suggests that teachers are slightly but significantly less likely to have positive expectations for ethnic-minority students, and direct less positive speech their way.[111]

Conversely, teachers may also be more likely to praise mediocre work from minority students,[112] either because they have different standards or with the intention of boosting the student's self-esteem.[113] This, however, can send the social cue that the teacher does not have high expectations for that student.

Some researchers are starting to explore how to start to flip these social cues on their heads, using a technique they refer to as 'wise' feedback. Although this research is still quite new and based on studies with fairly small sample sizes, it suggests a feedback approach that communicates high expectations of the student as an individual, and provides personal assurance that the teacher believes the student can reach them. For instance, students who received a note from their teacher stating, 'I'm giving you these comments because I have very high expectations and I know that you can reach them,' expressed higher trust that the school treated members of their ethnicity fairly, revised their essays more, and had higher grades, than students who received a control message.[114] [115]

What does this look like in the workplace? Performance feedback is a feature of most (hopefully all) workplaces. In the example at the beginning of the chapter, why did your heart sink when your boss started your feedback conversation with, 'Now, it's nothing to worry about, but ...'? Probably because his words and tone of voice suggested that he was worried, and was anticipating that you would get worried as well. Whatever is coming in your performance appraisal, it's not the kind of news that tends to have people jumping on the table cheering. How differently would that conversation have gone had your boss considered the cue he was sending and instead started with something like the 'wise' feedback above: 'Now, I'm giving you this feedback because I have high expectations that I know you can meet'? Perhaps you still wouldn't be jumping on the table, but at least you wouldn't be starting the conversation with your heart in your stomach.

Hearing the news that a nuclear waste dump is about to be built in your vicinity probably wouldn't have you cheering on the table either, but that is what happened to two communities in Switzerland in 1993. Projects like this typically fall under the category of 'Not In My Back Yard', or NIMBY. We might agree that it's good for there to be nuclear waste dumps, shopping malls, power plants, high-rise apartment blocks and council housing somewhere, but our enthusiasm dips markedly when it's close enough to impact on our quality of life (or the value of our house).

One obvious solution is to compensate people for the cost they are incurring – and if all that was on people's minds was money, then this would undoubtedly work. But, as we've already seen in this chapter, people can infer a great deal of social information even from something as seemingly economic as an offer of compensation. Bruno Frey and Felix Oberholzer-Gee,[116] two Swiss academics, explored whether people are more inclined to accept NIMBYish projects if they are compensated. In the two aforementioned Swiss communities, they interviewed 305 households – two thirds of the local population – to gauge their views on the potential building of the nuclear dump sites. Overall, slightly more than half the respondents were supportive of the facility, despite most respondents viewing it as a heavy burden for the community. At least, until they were offered compensation. Then the level of supportiveness halved to below a quarter of respondents. This finding has been replicated elsewhere.

So what are people inferring from the offer of compensation? One explanation could be that the compensation signals to people that the facility is more hazardous than they thought. Frey and Oberholzer-Gee reject this explanation based on the replies of the respondents. Instead, they argue that the cue being sent to communities is that this is an economic transaction, where they are being compensated for loss, rather than a civic arrangement. In these circumstances, people invariably find the compensation inadequate to the burden, and support falls.

The conclusion from this and the broader research on what is known as *motivational crowding out* (where extrinsic incentives, like money, 'crowd out' intrinsic motivation – our desire to do things for their own sake) is that the one social cue we want to try to avoid sending is that we don't think an individual has any reason of their own for engaging in a desired behaviour but instead must be regulated or incentivized into doing it.

Julian Le Grand, former UK Labour advisor and Professor of Social Policy at the London School of Economics, has explored this with regard to public sector professionals. He argues that the accountability structures around public services are designed with the expectation that the workers within them are either 'Knights' – intrinsically motivated professionals who will do the right thing and whose expertise should be respected – or 'Knaves', who will seek to extract as much benefit for themselves for as little effort as possible.[117] Of course, neither of these caricatures is found in its pure form in real life, and Le Grand argues that workers can become more knightish or knaveish depending on the cues they receive from the system around them. For instance, high levels of oversight, prescriptive rule-systems and regular auditing may make people feel that they are no longer trusted, which in turn causes them to act in less altruistic, more selfinterested ways. Essentially, if the organization views them as untrustworthy, then why should they act differently? Conversely, low levels of supervision and monitoring may make staff feel more trusted and motivated.

This is, however, not quite as straightforward as it sounds. The fact that workers feel trusted and motivated doesn't mean that they will act in a way that their managers or executives wish them to – they may have different priorities, preferences or information and in practice some supervision is generally necessary. For instance, in a job centre, a high level of autonomy for individual job coaches might result in similar claimants getting different outcomes based on who they see and what that job coach thinks is important. Or an individual doctor might wish to provide a patient with the most expensive form of care, but if every doctor made that decision it would have serious consequences for the overall sustainability of the healthcare system.

In these cases it seems to be important that workers acknowledge the legitimacy of the person or body providing the supervision, and of the rules that are being prescribed for them. The cue should be about supporting and trusting workers while providing some frameworks for their roles – not that they can't be trusted to do the right thing.

How people respond to the same cue will also depend on where they are in the organization. In the last chapter we looked at a study encouraging bankers to donate a day's salary to charity. Unsurprisingly, we found that telling staff that 7.5 per cent of all UK employees had donated had no effect on donation rates. But when we dug into the data we saw a more interesting pattern. People at the bottom of the bank's hierarchy were generally less likely to donate if they saw this social norm, but people at the top were about twice as likely to give if they saw the norm. Why is this? Perhaps these senior folks in the bank weren't responding to a social norm but rather to a signal that the fundraising campaign wasn't doing well, and that those in leadership roles needed to step up and do their bit.

Just as different groups of employees might respond to the same cue in different ways, some social groups may also respond differently to others. We know that marginalized groups also have to contend with the stream of social cues that are known as micro-aggressions, which wouldn't even register to the social instincts of a member of the dominant group. These small interactions, such as asking someone where they're from, asking them to repeat their name several times or commenting on their hair or dress, can act as constant reminders that a person is out of place or out of step with the dominant social groups. Over time, this may add up to a person feeling unwelcome in the environment, and can have effects on their work performance, retention and wellbeing.

But not all aggressions are 'micro'. It is impossible to forget that one of the social cues that some groups still receive is aggressive attention from law enforcement that says more about how they're expected to behave than how they have actually behaved.

Remember the broken windows theory? A statistical review, conducted in 2015 by Anthony Braga, Brandon Welsh and Cory Schnell, three American academics,[118] found that although trying to reduce the cues of social disorder (such as broken windows) had a modest effect on crime levels, more aggressive order-maintenance strategies (such as increasing police presence, detaining and searching more people) may have had the opposite effect. But why? The underpinning logic was the same: prevent low-level disorder and reduce the environmental cues that might lead to more serious crime. In the case of lighter-touch approaches, this seems to have been effective.

But it could be that social cues, while being the central idea of the policy, actually helped to undermine it in its more aggressive form. The stop-question-and-frisk programme employed in New York City, which did exactly what it said on the tin, was popular among the police and also with the city's then mayor, Michael Bloomberg, on the grounds that it stopped crime. At its peak, almost 700,000 people were subject to stop-question-and-frisk. The programme was also far from random, with widespread accusations of racial profiling and unarguably many more instances of black and Hispanic people, especially young men, being stopped – making it likely that during the eleven years the policy was active every young black man in New York had either been frisked himself or knew someone who had been.[119]

Stop-question-and-frisk was also notable for the lower threshold that officers needed to clear to be allowed to frisk someone. Before this policy, the police could frisk someone only after they had arrested them (and read them their rights), or if they had a search warrant. In New York, that threshold was lowered to 'reasonable suspicion' – essentially just the judgement of the police officer doing the searching.

Now, try and put yourself in the mind of a New Yorker who has either been searched or knows somebody who has – probably several somebodies, in fact. The police are stopping and searching hundreds of thousands of people a year, and have taken on special powers to do so. Does this seem like a cue of safety and order – a situation where crime is low? No: if crime was low, the police wouldn't need to do this, so crime must be *endemic* – everyone must be breaking the law. The police department had inadvertently telegraphed a social cue to a whole bunch of people who might not otherwise have been overly worried about crime in their area – or overly inclined to consider crime as an option themselves.

It's clear that social cues aren't always good, and they don't necessarily convey true information to influence our behaviour. In fact, we're so programmed to learn from patterns in our environment that we can often end up going down a route that isn't the best and doesn't actually reflect the desired or approved behaviour.

Here's another well-known example: Scared Straight. Scared Straight is a popular programme in the US and elsewhere that treats young people who are at risk of getting into trouble with the law to a 'prisoner for a day' experience, during which they're given talks (or shouted at) by prisoners and generally introduced to the likely consequences of their current actions.

Like stop-question-and-frisk, this seems like a good idea on the outside: juvenile delinquents don't understand how bad prison is; a good fright will set them back on the straight and narrow.

The problem is that Scared Straight not only doesn't work but may even make things worse. Young people who are sent on Scared Straight programmes are actually *more* likely to reoffend. Interestingly, none of the many evaluations that have now demonstrated the ineffectiveness of Scared Straight have been set up to understand *why* it doesn't work; and, damningly, some of them have been discontinued when the results started looking negative, shutting down any chance of understanding reasons for the backfire.[120]

However, researchers have come up with a few theories. Scared Straight might bring groups of at-risk teenagers into contact with each other, increasing the opportunities for negative peer-group formation; or targets may also display either an optimism bias (not believing they'll get caught) or might paradoxically be less worried about prison having experienced it (the fear of the unknown can be a powerful deterrent). However, another possible explanation has to do with the social cues we're sending to young people by taking them into prison. By treating at-risk young people like hardened criminals, perhaps we communicate to them that we expect them to become hardened criminals – a profoundly sad and toxic social cue. Interestingly, other studies have shown that any kind of contact with the formal criminal-justice system, even just official processing, can increase the likelihood of a person subsequently reoffending.[121]

As discussed earlier, it's worth considering, for example with people you line manage, or with colleagues or contractors, whether you're interacting with them in a way that sends a signal that you think they're bad or you're expecting things to go wrong. Simply approaching a situation with positive expectations ('How can we solve this together?') rather than negative ('How is this person going to let me down again?') can be a powerful way of changing the social cues you're sending.

Even if most of the cues in an environment aren't great, things can be improved by adding one, highly salient cue. Going back to Kees Keizer's study of people littering in the Netherlands, he found that the presence of someone sweeping the street and, as he puts it 'restoring order', significantly reduced people's tendency to litter, even in the 'messy' environment. When things have gone awry, and the social norm is perhaps skewed towards doing the wrong thing, changing the cue to show that doing the right thing is valued, even when it's difficult, can help give us a gentle push in the right direction.

In this chapter we've seen how small things in the environment, and the ways people interact, can give valuable social information about expected behaviour, even if that information isn't always what we intended to convey. When we're thinking about how to run a team, or build an organization, it pays to look at the little things as well as the big ones – because much of the time people will get their information about how to behave from the little cues in their environment rather than from the company's official policies. When it comes to social cues, it's actually useful to 'sweat the small stuff': thinking about clean-desk policies, dress codes (particularly for senior members of the team), or even what working hours you want people to keep (if your office is open 24/7, what cue does that send?) can be useful in making sure you end up with the kind of office culture you want. It's also helpful to ask staff members how they have interpreted the social cues they're receiving, and to listen to their responses. Your HR department answering questions from junior colleagues about, for example, how promotions work by referring to there being a policy will be unsatisfactory if those colleagues have observed policy being repeatedly ignored.

What is clear is that social groups are channels for information – about norms, expectations and beliefs – and that people within shared social groups actively seek to co-ordinate on the same norms, expectations and beliefs. In the next chapter we're going to explore how information flows through networks, and why people's beliefs can sometimes be so tricky to change.

8

Social Diffusion

'Where you sit in the cafeteria is crucial because you got everybody there. You got your Freshmen, ROTC Guys, Preps, JV Jocks, Asian Nerds, Cool Asians, Varsity Jocks, Unfriendly Black Hotties, Girls Who Eat Their Feelings, Girls Who Don't Eat Anything, Desperate Wannabes, Burnouts, Sexually Active Band Geeks, the greatest people you will ever meet, and the worst: beware of the Plastics.'

Janis, *Mean Girls*

S o, we know that people are highly influenced by the expectations of those in their social group, either as gleaned from a social norm or gathered from their interpretation of a cue. These influences can have meaningful real-world consequences if you're looking to design a policy, run a business or really just exist in the world in any way.

The previous phenomena are quite simple treatments, and take our social environment as it is – as if it doesn't change. But social groups aren't static and eternal: at some point they come into existence, and over time the 'ideal' member of the group, which sets the template for group behaviour, can change. To understand why this happens we need to understand *social diffusion* – how information spreads through social groups. Here, we're not talking about the way people respond to a pre-existing norm but rather the way in which norms are created, with a behaviour or information spreading from one person in the group to the rest of its members.

But how do we understand when someone is being influenced to change their behaviour or opinion, and what is the result of our tendency to prefer people with whom we already share social groups or other characteristics? Let's say that we look at people who are close to each other – friends or colleagues – and we see that lots of them share opinions or behaviours. Does that mean that some people are conforming to a pre-existing norm in a group they share, or that the behaviour has been passed from one person to another? If we can understand the way that behaviours are determined, we can understand how to shape and change them.

When BIT was in the UK government's Cabinet Office the entire team ate lunch together each day. Lunchtime social norms emerged – Simon's innovative strategy for getting as much custard as possible with his dessert became standard across the entire team, and thanks to some impromptu back-of-a-napkin calculations by Sam it was a fact universally acknowledged that eggs were a bad investment at the salad bar.* In this story, we know where an idea came from – Simon's love of custard, for example – but a lot of the ideas we share with our friends are harder to explain. If lots of your friends like *Star Wars*, and you like *Star Wars*, have your friends influenced you to like *Star Wars*? Or are you just more likely to be friends with people who like the same things as you?

---

* In the salad bar in the UK Treasury canteen, salads are charged for by weight. As the densest item that can be included, a boiled egg, though tasty, does not represent good value for money.

In the early 2000s, several groundbreaking research studies were published showing that a whole host of behaviours were 'socially contagious' – that we could catch them from our friends in the same way that we might catch a cold. Smoking, drinking and even obesity were found to be contagious in this way. In fact, the effects were so big that people started to get suspicious, and to take a deeper look at the statistics. The flaw in this analysis was uncovered when two two researchers used the same methodology to 'show' that height and ethnicity were contagious – which of course they are not.[122]

The problem with this kind of statistical analysis quickly became clear: people do not choose their friends at random, and we are attracted to people who are similar to ourselves. While the cliché 'opposites attract' might have some truth to it, the less catchy 'people who are broadly similar to each other in a number of characteristics attract' is probably more accurate.

Other teams in the Cabinet Office ate their lunches separately, either at different times or in different locations. This had noticeable effects on the amount of social diffusion that went on among those teams. They missed out on information from their colleagues – without Sam's intervention, for instance, we would never have known that televised StarCraft tournaments are a thing – but they also manage to avoid hours of discussion over what does and does not constitute a salad.*

---

* The definitive answer to this question is that a salad must contain at least two vegetable/fruit ingredients, and a colloid or dressing. This answer may not be completely satisfying, but represents a brokered peace between several factions of the team with very strong views. On the upside, a martini with olive and pimento counts as a salad, and is therefore an appropriate lunch for someone on a diet.

As BIT expanded, it became difficult for everyone to eat together, but most people still ate lunch as part of their teams. What got socially diffused therefore took on a new character. In the research team, we learned about the latest on the replication crisis in psychology, suggestions for podcasts, or the American National Public Radio feature 'Set Phasers to Poem'. In BI Ventures, which is home to 100 per cent of BIT's coeliac and vegan population, the topics of conversation might be very different. Some of this is not social diffusion but social selection – it's not a coincidence that BIT's nerdiest team also contains its biggest *Star Trek* fans – but there's definitely a diffusion element. Our colleague Charlotte, who headed up the BI Ventures arm, went from sedentary to athletic climber in the space of her two years at BIT, driven largely it seems by the profusion of climbers in her team. By contrast, Michael remains firmly rooted to the ground.

What we've described so far are examples of passive diffusion. Simon did not set out to convert us all to the custard-maximization solution, and David Halpern, BIT's CEO, did not set out to have one team of podcasting nerds and another of coeliac athletes – the social choice architecture of the team just arranged for this to happen. It doesn't have to be this way, though. Instead of being passive recipients of social diffusion, we can try to create it. We can become social choice architects.

This matters because diffusion is not limited to amusing though trivial things like *Star Trek* and custard. Norms and expectations, both good and bad, can diffuse from one person to another, and inside a team.

One team we worked with was a particularly good example of this. The team was dysfunctional – the deputy director hated the director, and everyone hated him. Working in a high-pressure area where results were important, there were often so many people trying to take credit for a success, or to dodge blame for a failure, that it was completely unclear who had done what.

Something that might have helped was some fresh blood, and thankfully this was easy to achieve. The rate of circulation of staff was naturally fairly high, with people moving from posting to posting and team to team all the time. Sure enough, after two years, the entire team had rotated out, and there was a completely new team from top to bottom. So, what happened to the team dynamic? Nothing changed at all – the team still hated and distrusted one another.

If you were overseeing this team, you would naturally ask why this happened. Is there perhaps something about the broader organization that is distrusting? Most teams have positive dynamics, so that can't be it. What about the area the team was working on? It was highly visible, so there was pressure, but not as much as there is in the Civil Contingencies Secretariat, for example, who plan for natural or other disasters and co-ordinate government efforts when there's flooding or terrorism.

Instead, the problem seems to have been about timing. This team ended up being a twist on the story of Theseus's ship. Theseus is a hero in Greek mythology whose ship was preserved to commemorate his heroism. Over the course of time, planks and other components of the ship began to warp or rot, and when that happened the ship's custodians, keen to maintain the monument, replaced each plank as it failed. Over the course of many years, every single aspect of the ship was replaced by fresh new planks. At that stage, was it really still the same ship?

Most of us would probably answer that it wasn't the same ship because it contained none of the same parts. Certainly, this is our favoured view – the new wood can't 'learn' from the old wood what it means to be a part of this ship, and the history of the ship isn't heritable. However, although we might describe a person as 'wooden' in their manner, they are (almost always) sentient and self-aware beings. So people *can* learn, and they can inherit.

Imagine that the team has twelve people in it, all of whom hate each other. Today, on the first day of the year, one person leaves and a new person arrives. This new person, let's call them Jemma, has been in the sector for a couple of years, and has just joined the organization. On day one, the deputy takes her to lunch and, although trying to be professional, struggles to give a glowing account of his boss, the director. What is Jemma to think? First of all, this puts a barrier between her and liking the director all that much, but it also may give her the impression that the deputy is a little bit bitter. Depending on how politic the deputy has (not) been, she may also assume that this is a team where gossip is rife.

Next, Jemma works on a project with another colleague at her level, and discovers that the colleague has taken credit for some of her work, or at least has not shared credit for joint work. Within a couple of weeks, she quickly comes to learn that the director isn't well regarded, that the deputy isn't loyal to his boss, may be bitter and is potentially a gossip, and that there's a culture of taking credit for things others have done. She may not hate everyone else in the team, but it's early days yet; and she's certainly not that trusting of her colleagues, and may decide that she is best served by keeping herself to herself and making sure that she gets her fair share of the credit. Because of the psychological bias of overconfidence, coupled with the salience of her own work, she may be wrong about what share of the credit is 'rightfully' hers. Within a couple of weeks, one plank in the ship has been slotted into place, and 'learned' from the other planks around it what kind of ship this is.

Another two weeks down the line, another member of the team leaves and is replaced by a new person, Sunil. Sunil arrives and goes through the same process as Jemma, but this time he's also buddied up with Jemma, as she's also new and can teach him the ropes. Jemma, who is still a kind-hearted person, tells Sunil about her concerns about the dynamics in the team and the apportionment of credit. Sunil is therefore on the same path as Jemma, but this is accelerated by her telling him about her experiences.

Another month later, one more person leaves and another one joins – Harriet. Harriet has the same experience as Sunil, but is buddied with *him*, and so gets the benefit of his experience and Jemma's. Harriet is then assigned to work on a project with Jemma, by this stage a more experienced member of the team; and, when the time comes to present the project's findings, she discovers that Jemma, influenced by her own experiences, has taken most of the credit for the work done.

Fast-forward nine more months into this programme and you have a brand-new team – a whole new ship – which has none of the same people as the original team, but all of the same problems. Unless there's a single rotten element, excising one part of the rot won't have the desired effect.

This dynamic need not be an unpleasant one – we could just as easily have told a story with a virtuous circle as we could a vicious one. But even in the case of a very well-integrated team, there are things to look out for. *Groupthink*, first studied by the Yale psychologist Irving Janis around the time of the Bay of Pigs disaster, can easily infect teams where people like each other and where there is a social norm of agreement. In that sort of environment, bad ideas are thought to be good – or at least nobody challenges the cosy consensus, even if they believe it's wrong. As we've seen from famous conformity experiments such as those carried out by Solomon Asch in the 1950s, people are reluctant to speak up even when they're in a room with a group of strangers. How much can we be influenced by people who we're living on top of for a year?

The study that first looked at this rigorously was carried out by Bruce Sacerdote at Dartmouth College in the 1990s. Sacerdote found that roommate assignment – the selection of who lives with who during their first year in college – wasn't made by the students but instead happened at random. That meant that a punk-rock enthusiast could be paired with a classical cellist, or an American-football player paired with a student for whom aggressive sports with commercial breaks every three minutes were boring. Thanks to the proximity that American college life forces students into for that first year, these potentially very different young people had to spend a lot of time in each other's company, and Sacerdote was able to work out how powerful social diffusion is using a clean test.

What he found was quite striking. Students who had been paired together had more similar grades than could be explained by chance, were both more likely to join fraternities and more likely to join the same fraternity. These effects were quite modest – if your roommate's average grade was one unit higher (the equivalent of moving from about average to a top-performing student) then your score would be 0.12 units higher (enough to go from about average to the top 35 per cent of students) – but they were real, and seemed to persist, albeit with some shrinkage, until the end of a student's time at college.

The Sacerdote study was groundbreaking, tackling the difficult problem of identifying the causal effects of social diffusion in an elegant way. However, it's also a rare case of the published academic literature giving us an *underestimate* of the true size of the power of a phenomenon.

His research design is neat – randomly assigning people to roommates gives us a clear picture – but it doesn't accurately reflect the way that we normally form relationships, which is often much more systematic. We form relationships based on the chance of geography and timing, of course, but we don't find ourselves where we are in life – either personally, professionally or geographically – by chance alone. Take this book, for example – it has two authors, who were born on opposite sides of the planet. We are writing it together because we're friends, and we're friends because of work. How did we get there? We both studied social science, and are interested in public policy and the myriad ways that economics fails to explain human behaviour. At BIT, we worked together on education projects, because that's an area of policy we're both interested in. The fact that this book has been written is a good case study in Michael influencing Susannah's behaviour.

The point is, people we have less social distance from – for example, people with whom we have something in common, or already share a history – are better at influencing us than people who are more socially remote. Random assignment – assigning people to different roommates based on the flip of a coin, or a computer's random number generator – makes for good research, but means that we miss out on this. In the same way, if we're thinking about using social influence to nudge people, we shouldn't expect it to work just as well everywhere – in places where people are more closely connected, or have had a lot of choice in who is in their networks, we think that nudges will diffuse more quickly, and more completely, than if people's networks are much more governed by random chance or an arbitrary assignment.

In Chapter 6 we looked at the study we ran at a large investment bank, as part of the bank's annual fundraising drive, where a social norm of 7.5 per cent of people donating did not increase donations except among senior managers. The bank ran this campaign every year and it worked like a well-oiled machine. The bank's employees were asked to donate a day's salary to charity – quite a bit of money, in some cases. The campaign took place over a single day, and all the money raised went to two charities chosen by the bankers themselves. Everyone was emailed by the corporate social responsibility department and asked to donate, which they could do by simply clicking a link in the email, going to a website, or scanning their bank ID badge with a modified scanner carried by fundraisers going around the building.

For this campaign, however, we varied something – some people were randomly assigned to receive a personal email from the bank's CEO. The emails were sent using a mail merge, so it wasn't as though the CEO was actually emailing people personally, but they were addressed to the person in question, so 'Dear Jo' rather than the 'Dear Colleague' email coming from the CSR department.

The results of the experiment were impressive – with about twice as many people who received the personal email donating compared to those that received the impersonal one. But what's really interesting is the pattern that we see in the results and how they vary depending on the seniority of the person being emailed.

What we see is that the people at both the top and bottom of the company are much more influenced than the people in the middle by the personal email. This makes sense and is consistent with what we've seen in previous chapters. Analysts – the people at the bottom of the bank – probably never receive an email from the CEO, so this feels pretty special, even if they can probably work out that it's been automated. As you get more senior in the bank, this effect goes down, because you probably get more emails from the CEO. However, there's another effect heading in the opposite direction. The people at the top of the bank, the grandly titled managing directors (of which there are still several hundred in the bank's UK office) are socially much closer to the CEO – they've definitely met him, have been to meetings with him and might even get genuinely personal emails from him. They're less impressed by the email, but it's probably more meaningful to them because of the lower social distance between them and the CEO. People in the middle of the bank have neither of these – they get enough emails from the CEO that another one doesn't matter that much, but they don't have any personal connection to him either.

The CEO might be the most important person in a company, but they might not be the most influential on a person-by-person basis. Consider your boss's boss's boss: how much time do you spend thinking about what they want, what they would do in a situation, or how they are likely to respond to something? Now think about *your* boss: how much more time do you spend thinking about them in the same ways? Or the other way around: how much mental energy do you invest in your direct reports, compared to how much you invest in *their* direct reports?

We're starting to see more active diffusion (an idea wilfully flowing from the CEO to junior staff; Michael actively trying to convince Susannah to write a book) but it's really only one space removed from the types of passive diffusion (where information or behaviours come to be shared by members of a group without anyone intending to influence anyone else) that we've seen in previous chapters.

How, then, are we going to see what social diffusion is capable of, when we give it a chance to really fly? Most research in this area, like Sacerdote's, involves forming social groups at random and seeing what happens to the outcomes you're interested in. To see the real power of social diffusion, we should find a network that already exists and see what happens when we change part of it.

Over the last few years, behavioural scientists have tried to do just that. The idea is quite simple, despite being logistically hard to pull off. You find an established social network and map it – this gives you a sense of the lie of the land, and who is connected to who. You then find one node in a network (also known as a person) and do something to that node. Because you've targeted your intervention, you can then see what happens to everyone else.

At BIT, we ran one of the first experiments in this area, collaborating with Michael Norton from Harvard Business School. Our idea was to try to find a sweet spot in those social influences previously discussed. The more senior someone is, the more powerful an influence they should be; but the more socially remote they are, the less of an impact we expect to see. Middle managers, we reasoned, are both senior and socially close, so maybe they'd be the most effective influencers?

We worked with a large employer, again using a large one-day fundraising campaign as the basis for our experiment.[123] A quarter of the firm's employees got business as usual – another standard email from the corporate social responsibility department asking them to donate. For another quarter of the employees, we also emailed the vice president of their business unit and thanked them for their support of the campaign – essentially increasing the dose on prominent individuals to see whether passive influence like this can spread. For the next quarter of employees, we sent the vice president an email and asked them to 'reach out to your colleagues in your business unit and ask them to donate'. Finally, the fourth quarter got a similar email, but in which we tried to put words in the mouths of the vice presidents, saying:

> *Please reach out and email your colleagues in your business unit, and let them know about the huge contribution their donation can make.*

We call this kind of an intervention a 'network nudge' – trying to have an effect not just on the individual but also on other people in their network. The emails went out at 8.30 in the morning, and we followed the donations made by people during the day of the campaign and until donations had petered out. What we found was surprising to the point where, years later, Michael still returns to the dataset regularly to try to find an error in his earlier work. But so far it has held up.

In the control group – those people who were emailed just by the CSR department – about 6 per cent of people donated to charity. In the second group, where people's managers were sent a thank-you email, the rate of donation went up to 12 per cent – roughly doubling as a result of this kind of passive social influence. It was in the network-nudge group that things became astonishing. In the first network-nudge condition – where managers were asked to reach out – 24 per cent of people donated: a huge increase from the 12 per cent in the 'thanks' group. In the 'impact group', where we had tried to put words in the mouths of vice presidents, it went still higher, to 39 per cent. We raised as much money from this group as we did from the other three groups together – almost half a million pounds. How did this happen?

Looking at the data, what we see is that the donations in the business units that got either of the network-nudge messages happened at about the same time of day – or at least much closer together in time than they had in the other groups. Basically, it looked like the vice presidents stood up in their packed offices and said, 'Right – we're all going to do this, right now.' That's a hugely powerful thing.

Incredulous about these findings, we wanted to find another opportunity to test them. Thankfully, we didn't have to wait long. In 2013, David Cameron, the then Prime Minister of the United Kingdom, had stood in front of Number 10 and said that the rise of dementia among Britain's ageing population constituted a crisis and that the new Dementia Friends programme, which would educate people about how to spot dementia and to help afflicted family and friends, would recruit one million 'friends' by the time of the next election, in 2015. Fast-forward to summer 2014, less than a year until the next election, and only about 75,000 had been recruited. Something else had to be done.

Recruiting dementia friends was a two-step process. First, 'dementia champions' were recruited. These dementia champions needed to undertake a day's training about dementia and how to spot it, what to do about it and so on. Champions were then responsible for recruiting others to attend one- or two-hour training events – and those people would in turn become 'dementia friends'.

In some ways, the programme had been a success. It had recruited 10,000 dementia champions – exactly what was expected. The challenge was that the champions were recruiting far fewer friends than anticipated – only about seven each at the time we started working with the charity.

So dementia champions were responsible for recruiting people to become friends, but had failed to do so – in fact, most of them had never run a single event, and so beyond their initial training may not have been engaged at all.

We ran our experiment on 427 dementia champions who had been recruited but had so far not run any sessions. All of these champions were emailed and offered advice on how to run sessions to recruit dementia friends. A third of the champions were also sent a network-nudge message suggesting that they ask their friends and family to become dementia friends. And another third were sent a 'second degree' network-nudge message, requesting that champions 'ask their friends and family to ask their friends to become dementia friends' – explicitly trying to increase the rate of diffusion through the champions' network.

A few months later, the results were in. We found that even the follow-up email had been pretty successful – champions in the control group recruited an average of eight friends each, having recruited none previously. In the network-nudge condition we found another encouraging effect of active social diffusion: champions there recruited an average of sixteen friends – double the number recruited with only the basic email. In the second-degree condition, champions recruited … eight friends each. Half as much as in the first network condition, and the same number achieved with only the basic email. We had tried to dial up the intervention, but the effect disappeared.

So what happened? Well, imagine you're on the other end of that email. You know someone who has dementia, so you've signed up as a dementia champion and you're intending to run an event. You receive an email that encourages you to do so, and suggests you reach out to your friends via social media to get things started. Great: you do so, your friends turn up and the event is a huge success.

But imagine instead you receive an email asking you to reach out to your friends and get them to reach out to their friends. That's a bit different. Probably the threshold of friendship required is higher because you're asking your friends to contribute their own social influence to your undertaking – and it does start to sound a little bit like a pyramid scheme. So you reach out to fewer, closer friends. And they, in turn, reach out to fewer friends because they're not as concerned about dementia awareness as you are.

In lots of groups there are strong taboos against certain topics – the classic 'no religion or politics at the dinner table', for example – and norms often dictate what it's appropriate to ask for support with. It turns out that asking your friends to invite their friends to a dementia-awareness event probably amounts to having a bit of an awkward conversation, and people need a little more help to have awkward conversations.

In the UK, 16.4 per cent of adults are not confident reading and writing and even more – 24 per cent – are not confident with maths.[124] For the US, these figures are 17.5 and 28.7 per cent respectively.[125] For people who are not confident in their reading and writing, in particular, their struggle not only affects their ability to navigate everyday life but is often also a source of embarrassment or even shame. From 2014 to 2017, BIT ran a research centre called the Behavioural Research Centre for Adult Skills and Knowledge (ASK), the remit of which was to explore how we could get people into, and through, foundational English and mathematics courses.

However, an immediate barrier we faced was that, because of the stigma associated with poor English and maths skills, people did not want to come forward and sign up for training. We found that a lot of employers were willing to support their staff in improving these skills, but that staff were nonetheless reluctant to put their hands up because they thought it might negatively affect their employment. An additional obstacle for many people was that their experience of compulsory education had been characterized by failure; they did not anticipate that returning to learning would be enjoyable.

The first trial Susannah ever ran at BIT was with Lincolnshire Co-Operative (a UK grocery-store chain) and was a notable failure. We attached fliers to staff payslips, emphasizing either the intrinsic benefits or the financial benefits of improving their mathematical skills. Of the more than 2,000 people in the trial, less than twenty-five in total responded across the two conditions. Back to the drawing board.

Next, Susannah worked with Transport for London to encourage people to approach the TfL training team about course opportunities. We'd already tried something similar to the Lincolnshire Co-Operative trial with TfL, with similarly underwhelming results. Now we were interested in testing the same sort of network nudge previously described: we wanted to see if people who were unlikely to respond to a direct offer from the training team might be more likely to respond to an approach from a colleague who had already done a course.

Accordingly, we divided TfL staff up into organizational units – stations and depots – where at least one staff member had completed a course at the Learning Zone in the past two years. This gave us 49 organizational units with more than 8,000 staff in total. We then devised a set of emails to send out to the former learners. The control group received no email; the first group were sent an email thanking them for attending the Learning Zone and inviting feedback; the second group were sent an email in which they were thanked and asked to reach out to any colleague they thought could benefit from attending a course; and the third group were sent an email in which they were thanked, asked to reach out to colleagues and informed that anyone who signed up for a course in the next three months would go into the draw to win one of ten Amazon vouchers.

Dear Joe

Your friends and colleagues could win prizes totalling £1,000 if they sign up to a class at the Learning Zone

I wanted to congratulate you on completing a qualification in English at the TfL Learning Zone on 20 July.

Please take a moment to think about how completing this course has influenced your life – have you become more confident? More able to manage your time and money, communicate with colleagues, or operate a computer? Has it opened up new professional and personal opportunities?

If so, please reach out and let your friends and colleagues know about the value of the course. I would love to see them at the Learning Zone sometime soon.

Your friends or colleagues will be entered into a prize draw to win prizes totalling £1,000 if they sign up for any of our classes by 30 November.

Anyone who works for TfL can attend the Learning Zone and it's easy to find out more about courses. Just tell them to email [email].

Thanks for your help,

Ashraf, Learning Zone Manager

Interestingly, we saw no significant difference in sign-up rates across the first three conditions (the control, 'thanks' and 'reach'), even though in previous trials we'd found that asking people to reach out to friends could work. But when we added the prize, almost four times as many people enquired about courses. It's clear that offering the prize changed the basis of the conversation between colleagues from 'Hey, I think you could benefit from some training' to 'Hey, the Learning Zone is offering a prize to people who sign up for courses', which is a much easier opener for a tricky conversation.

Consistent with this, Rachel Gershon, a PhD student in

marketing at Washington University, explored the effects of different kinds of incentives on customer referrals and found that prosocial incentives consistently outperform selfish incentives, for two reasons: first, it's much easier (and more appealing) to encourage a friend to sign up to something that benefits them rather than you; and second, the friend is the one who encounters the friction of signing up (or switching), so it's useful to incentivize them to follow through.[126]

More evidence of the importance of considering how to facilitate conversations comes from our work with a large international charity, which we helped with their fundraising. The charity runs an annual campaign one month every year, in the run-up to Christmas, but some keen beans will donate beforehand – in 2015, 292 people donated in the two weeks before the campaign started. Since they'd sought out the charity to donate before the main push, we suspected they were highly engaged with the organization, and could potentially be encouraged to get their friends to donate as well.

In this study, we had three conditions: a basic network-nudge email encouraging donors to reach out to their friends; a simple matched donation, where if the friend donated we'd match their donation up to £10; and a threshold-matched donation, where if the friend donated £50 we'd contribute a £10 donation. The friend also had to donate before the campaign started on the end of the main campaign – 31 December.

We allocated each donor a code that their friend had to input in order to get the match, which allowed us to track which friends belonged to which original donors.

Overall, the basic network nudge resulted in no additional donations, suggesting in this case that a network nudge, even with highly engaged donors, did not cause them to encourage their friends – or at least not quickly. Perhaps this was because the time-specific nature of the campaign made it strange for people to talk to their friends about it outside of the month of December itself, a bit like sending a Christmas card in March.

However, the simple match resulted in significantly more donations (donors in this condition were 12.5 percentage points more likely to generate donations from their network) compared to the control. So being able to tell your friends their donation will go further if they do it in the next few days has a significant impact.

The threshold match did not significantly increase donations, but those who did donate donated roughly twice as much as those in the simple-match condition (an average donation of £22 versus £45). Particularly interesting in terms of social diffusion is the fact that none of the donations in the threshold-match condition were generated by donors who had donated less than £50 themselves. It turns out that another awkward conversation to have is asking your friends to donate more than you've donated yourself – so if we're trying to get behaviours to diffuse through a network, we should be careful not to ask people to encourage their friends to do something they haven't done themselves.

In the last five chapters we've looked at the social choice architecture of our environments – how we identify with others, and how those identities shape our behaviours; how we respond to prevailing norms, often unconsciously; how the cues in our environment steer us towards particular actions; and how information and action moves from one person in a network to others. We've also focused on how these findings from behavioural science can be not only understood but also used to change our environments, and the behaviours that they elicit, for the better.

As the limitations of network nudges show us, tinkering with the architecture and nudging people in the right direction can take us only so far. Some things won't move well through a network, and sometimes the networks we need don't exist or aren't being put to good use. To overcome this, we're going to need to look beyond nudges to more fundamental questions about social capital – the essential building blocks of our networks.

PART 3

Networks

9

Social Capital

'It's not what you know; it's who you know that matters.'

Proverb

OES IT EVER feel like the world's a very small place, and that everyone knows everyone? In part, advances in technology make this true; but it's probably also because, while the world may be big, we move in small circles within it. When Michael went to a meeting at the Deputy Prime Minister's office a few years ago, shortly after Susannah had joined the Behavioural Insights Team, he was surprised to discover that the person sitting opposite him, Carmel, already knew Susannah, having worked with her in Australia. This was, as it turned out, because she had done a four-month job swap there in the same government department as Susannah – a coincidental overlap that came back around only by chance years later. More coincidental still, the swap was with Susannah's colleague Luke, whose partner Kate is the principal policy advisor leading the State of Victoria's Behavioural Insights Unit. Kate would have independently arrived on our radar as a leader in the international behavioural insights movement – except that Michael had already known Kate from when she took a behavioural science class he was involved in at the Harvard Kennedy School. When

Michael visited Melbourne in 2018 and Kate was the first person to babysit his son.

Robert Putnam, the Harvard professor who has come to be known as the 'poet laureate of civil society', defines social capital as 'connections among individuals – social networks and the norms of reciprocity and trustworthiness that arise from them'. That's a good definition, and one that will get you top marks in an exam if you were asked 'What is social capital?'. But what does Putnam actually mean?

In his seminal book, *Bowling Alone*, he measures social capital in part through things that shed some light on the substance of what it is: the number of family dinners we have together, sat around the table, which are a measure of how much parents are investing in their children; and participation in social and civic organizations like clubs and societies, political parties or charities.

Slightly confusingly, family dinners and being members of a social club are both the consequence of social capital – prompting Putnam to use them as indicators – and among the causes of social capital. Putnam's work is largely concerned with measuring whether one society or another has social capital, and whether that social capital changes over time. In *Bowling Alone*, he charted the decline of American social capital over the generations. The inspiration for the title comes from a single, stark finding. Although more people in the US were bowling than before, they were less likely to do so as part of a team or league. People are presumably, therefore, still enjoying bowling, and they're probably spending, if anything, slightly more money on bowling. So there's nothing to suggest that their economic capital is declining. But their social capital, which emerged from the bowling leagues and the people they met, has been lost.

The associations between social capital at the societal level, fuelling democratic participation and the strength of institutions, reducing corruption and increasing economic growth, make it too important for governments to ignore, and the implicit call to action from Putnam – that we should do something about the decline in social capital – has been taken up on both sides of the Atlantic, providing some of the inspiration for Britain's National Citizen Service (on which more later), and AmeriCorps in the US.

As with any type of capital, there's quite a lot of variability in how much people have. Some people make connections easily, have a lot of opportunities to meet lots of people and are very well networked. Importantly, perhaps they were born into a family or a position in society that gave them an in-built cache of social capital.

At the extreme end of this, we can think of someone like Prince Harry, the youngest son of Charles, Prince of Wales, and sixth in line to the British throne. Prince Harry could not really have been born into a more prestigious family, nor one with better access to resources and connections.[127] In addition, he appears by all accounts to be an affable and likeable man, meaning that he can make friends easily, with his status as a prominent royal, providing networking opportunities while working in his official capacity.

But it is also clear that Harry has put that capital to good use. He served as guest editor of the *Today* programme on BBC Radio 4 in December 2017[128] – an opportunity undeniably only available to him because of the circumstances of his birth. Editing *Today*, one of the most widely listened to radio programmes in Britain, allowed him to focus on topics that were of interest to him – mental health, climate change and the armed forces.[129] In talking about climate change, he interviewed Prince Charles, a long-standing conservationist, who is also of course his father.

A bigger coup, however, was interviewing Barack Obama in his first interview since leaving presidential office nearly a year earlier. It is difficult to argue that this is purely a consequence of Prince Harry's title and position. By this time Obama was out of office and had no need to curry favour with the British establishment, nor with the sixth in line to the throne. Instead, it seems that Harry was using his royal status – which had led him to meet the Obamas in 2015 on an official visit to the US and later appeared in videos with them to promote the Invictus Games[130] – to help further the causes he cares about. The prince may have been given an enormous initial endowment of social capital, but has done a better job than many at actually putting it to use.

It is, of course, very difficult for most of us to relate to the blue-blooded, TV-star-marrying, former-wild-child-turned-national-treasure Prince Harry, and there is a lot of evidence that the difference between you and him is probably getting wider.

In *Bowling Alone*, and later in *Our Kids*, Putnam memorably contrasted the town of his birth – Port Clinton, Ohio – over time. His classmates, decades ago, may have been divided economically but had roughly equal access to opportunities and social capital that allowed them a good chance of upward mobility. The Port Clinton of the twenty-first century is very different – with opportunity for progression, and social capital, much more deeply divided than before.

Putnam's so-called 'scissor' diagrams show the pattern, with things getting better over time for the well-off, and worse for those who already had little. Although these figures can be depressing, they show that things can change over time and that maybe, if we're a bit smarter in how we think about helping people with low social capital, we can reverse the trend of rising inequality.

A great example of the importance of both economic and social capital can be found in the US Department of Housing and Urban Development's Moving to Opportunity (MTO) programme, one of the largest and most expensive randomized controlled trials ever conducted. In MTO, thousands of families were given vouchers that allowed them to move from typically low-quality social-housing projects to nicer, more expensive accommodation in different neighbourhoods.[131]

MTO was ambitious and went beyond simply providing families with money to help them improve their lot in life, or make incremental improvements in their housing stock. The act of moving families from high-poverty to lower-poverty areas disrupts not just their physical and economic capital but also their social capital – the people they know, where their children go to school and the kind of life they can imagine for themselves.

The early results from the evaluation – the most rigorous ever conducted with a government programme like this – were mixed. No effects were seen on educational or economic outcomes during the first decade or so, but health and happiness improved for the families that received the vouchers. At about the same time, another analysis from MTO showed that the behaviour and aspirations of young women who had moved were positively affected, although it's not clear why it worked particularly for that group.

In the short term, then, the benefits were primarily on the social, and not the economic end. Later analysis, conducted by Harvard's Raj Chetty and his colleagues, showed that there *were* economic and educational gains, but that these were present only for those children who had moved as part of the programme before they turned thirteen. For children who moved after this point, the effects weren't just smaller; they were actually negative. The disruption of being moved from their original neighbourhood and their established social capital did these older children more harm than the new neighbourhood, with all its benefits, did good.

This finding points to some of the major differences between social and economic capital, at least in our view: social capital can't be easily transferred between individuals in the same way that money can (through redistributive taxes) and improving our stock of social capital often doesn't mean supplementing it, but can mean tearing it down and starting again. Think about the research on 'acting white' (see Chapter 2), and the very real fear of punishment from within people's own community for attempting to leave it.

If we take these facts together, we see another difference between what poverty means in an economic and a social-capital sense. People living in poverty have, by definition, low or no income, and may have no or even negative wealth.[132] However, with a few exceptions, they're unlikely to be devoid of social capital – they still have a family and friends. According to Putnam's research, they might actually have *more* social capital than their more affluent peers. Putnam associates social capital with things like attending church, which is more prevalent among people with lower incomes, and he controversially finds that people who live in more diverse communities are also lower in social capital. In many parts of the world, including rural south-west England where Michael is from, lower incomes and homogeneously white communities are common, so Putnam would expect them to be low in economic capital but high in social capital – and yet aspirations and mobility are low.

In these cases, the problem isn't so much a lack of social capital but more that social capital may be inefficiently deployed, or may not itself be connected to the networks that are needed to make it useful. From an outside, societal point of view, this will look like a person having low social capital, and the society being poorer for it, but at the individual level things look a bit different.

Our individual networks can end up looking a bit like the Australian railway network. Because each state was free to set their own railway standards, the majority of states functioned on different gauges, necessitating changing trains at state borders and adding friction to rail travel across an already vast country. Each state could be well connected within itself, but the country as a whole was disconnected, which makes a big difference when you consider that Australia's biggest cities are all in different states and at least 500 miles away from each other.*

Nobel-prizewinning economist Amartya Sen grew up in Bengal in the 1930s and 1940s and saw first-hand the ravages of famine – something he later studied in his career as an economist. One of the things that he found was that famines could not be explained simply by a lack of food. Sen identified that, as well as war, politics and British misrule of India, food simply couldn't get to where it was needed due to a lack of informed and interested central co-ordination and infrastructure. In many cases, the roads and rails needed to move food around were lacking or simply didn't exist.

---

* Had the Proclaimers started in Melbourne and walked 500 miles they would just about have made it to Sydney, but another 500 miles would have landed them somewhere in the wilderness south of Brisbane (Australia's third biggest city).

Just as food and other vital resources can't be transported within an infrastructure network that is disconnected (like Australia) or doesn't go where it needs to (like India), a lack of social capital means you can't get the things that you need to get on in life or to function in society from wherever they are to wherever you are, through your social network.

From an individual perspective, then, social capital comes down less to whether you are a member of a civic organization or have family dinners together and more, as the Ghostbusters might ask, to 'Who're you going to call?'

If we, the authors, have a thorny problem at work, we generally call each other on the way home to talk about it. If we need to know which gin to buy someone for their birthday, our colleague Louise is a useful source of advice, while our colleague Jess is a source of wisdom on all the coolest coffee shops in basically every city in Britain. Michael knows that for all plumbing-related worries he should call his mother, while his wife's friend's husband Mark is the go-to for almost anything else practical. If you're looking for a quick way to measure your social capital, you can think about how many different situations you can find solutions to by calling a friend, or a friend of a friend, and asking their advice or their support, without needing to actually spend money to fix it.

If we take this definition, then Putnam's use of membership – be it of a bowling club or a political party – as a proxy for social capital makes sense. The Freemasons, although by nature secretive, is an organization rich in social capital. Its members always seem to have someone they can call – an accountant, someone who owns a van company or a fleet of buses, a landscape gardener, a roofer, a restaurant proprietor or a solicitor – who can be helpful if you ever need any of those things. It doesn't seem like any of this happens for free, but it might happen at mates' rates, and it makes some services easier to access than they would otherwise have been.

We also know that the benefits of group membership can extend beyond borders. One of our former colleagues visited the UK from the US to work as a research assistant for the summer, and her parents were worried about her travelling across an ocean and living in a strange town. They reached out to their rabbi, who in turn reached out to a rabbi he had trained with and who now worked in London, who put our friend in touch with a family he knew, so that she arrived with pre-made friends and a support network. In fact, she became so close to the family that this year she's marrying their son.

Our natural instinct is to interpret this as a story about how it is, indeed, a small world after all.* But even if we don't all begin our lives well-networked in government or academia, once you're in a group social capital tends to build around you like moss on a stone.

It should be obvious that having social capital can be a powerful benefit in the world of work. In fact, social capital is what underlies the quote at the beginning of the chapter – that *who* you know matters more than *what* you know. Have you ever taken a job at a place someone you knew already worked? Or had a friend forward you a role they thought you might like? Or asked advice from a friend or family member about how to deal with a work problem? Indeed, we are often told that collecting and cultivating social capital (called 'networking', usually with a pained eye-roll)

---

* To quote the worst of the rides at Disney World.

is vital to our professional success. Dale Carnegie's book *How to Win Friends and Influence People* is essentially a handbook for building professional social capital. People who have a great deal of social capital in the workplace tend to be known as deal-makers or movers and shakers. They're well spoken-of, have the ears of decision-makers and know who to call to get that invoice fast-tracked or that issue with the shipment resolved.

Many people these days collect their professional social capital via a platform like LinkedIn, which allows us to maintain weak social ties with those we've crossed paths with – and sometimes this circles around to be useful. For example, when a former colleague of Susannah's who founded a start-up messaged her via the site for behavioural insights advice.

But how do you join a network in the first place? Here we turn to a piece of cultural anthropology that is the TV show *Gilmore Girls*, about mother and daughter Lorelai and Rory Gilmore. If we confine ourselves to the original series and not to the Netflix sequel, the story of Rory Gilmore appears to be one of social mobility. Having attended Stars Hollow High at the outset of the series, she moves to Chilton, an elite preparatory school, and from there to Yale and, on graduating from college, to work as a journalist following the fledgling presidential campaign of Barack Obama. Along the way, she becomes a member of the Daughters of the American Revolution (DAR).

This last fact is the loose thread on which we can pull to unravel the story of Rory Gilmore, social climber. Membership of the DAR is hereditary; to join, one must be female (hence the name) and a direct descendant of people directly involved in the American War of Independence against Britain. Although not all of the organization's 185,000 members are drawn from the upper stratum of American society, the membership as portrayed in *Gilmore Girls* certainly are.

Rory's access to Chilton comes about because she's smart, yes, but also because her grandparents are paying for it. The same goes for Yale, her grandfather's alma mater, for which the elder Gilmores pay until Rory's absent father picks up the tab following a large inheritance. Rory's first meaningful experience of Yale, having intended to go to Harvard, was a meeting with the Dean of Admissions, set up by her grandfather. In fact, the only blip in Rory's upward trajectory comes when she steals a boat, is caught, sentenced to community service and temporarily drops out of Yale. Viewed in the round, it seems that Rory's mother Lorelai is the outlier of the Gilmore family, having rejected her parents' privilege in her teens, and that Rory's mobility is more accurately thought of as a return to the status quo for her family. When we combine Lorelai's unwavering support for her daughter, the love of the townspeople of Stars Hollow, and her grandparents' access to both economic and social capital, Rory's success seems like a done deal from the outset.

Rory's boyfriends are *much* more interesting, however. Over the course of the seasons there are three worth writing about – Dean, Jess and Logan. The first, Dean, starts off as the sweet local boy from Stars Hollow and ends up as the most universally condemned of the three having left neither Stars Hollow nor the career path he was on at the beginning of the show as a junior at Stars Hollow High. Throughout the show, Dean's social capital is confined to Stars Hollow itself, and his economic capital is limited (he drops out of college to take on extra work and moves back in with his parents following his divorce).

Logan, the last of the boyfriends, is drawn from the other end of the spectrum. He's the son of a newspaper magnate and thinks nothing of flying to New York from Connecticut by helicopter at short notice. On the social capital side, Logan's parents are well connected, and his mother is a member of the DAR. When we first meet Logan, he's a member of a Yale secret society whose members seem to be similarly moneyed and connected. Yet as different as Logan is from Dean, they share a common characteristic: a lack of progress. Logan starts rich, connected and aloof, and ends if anything richer and more connected (although perhaps a little less aloof).

The poster boy for social capital, however, is Jess.* Jess arrives in Stars Hollow with no capital, either economic or social. His mother has turfed him out and sent him to live with his uncle, Luke Danes, presumably in response to the fact that Jess starts the story as an unruly shit. Moving to Stars Hollow doesn't do much to improve his economic prospects, but it does bring about two important changes to his social capital. First, meeting Rory (and being tutored by her) helps his education and lets him see a world beyond the path he first imagined he was on. Second, and more importantly, his guardianship transfers from his mother – who is scatty and itinerant – to Luke Danes, the model of a solid and dependable figure. By the end of the show, Jess has moved to New York and set up a publishing house with some friends. He hasn't reached the dizzying heights of Logan's success, but – thanks to social capital – he's come further than either of the others.

Although older, Jess resembles most closely the children who benefited most from MTO – he had no networks to disrupt, and

---

* Full disclosure: we're both #teamjess.

so movement to a better environment was more beneficial than it was harmful.

By now you've probably recognized some of the sources of social capital in your life: your parents and their generation, who helped you with homework, gave you advice about where to apply for study and work and told you stories about their jobs that gave you an idea of what the world of work was like. Your friends, who provide support and comfort and may have put you forward for a job, put you in touch with people they know in your city or have fixed your sink, given you legal advice or booked you travel with their employee discount. And your colleagues, who have gone on to other jobs but stayed in touch, and whose expanding networks can become your networks via a simple, 'I think we have a mutual colleague ...'

But what happens if, unlike Jess from *Gilmore Girls*, we feel comfortable and safe inside our current networks, even if they're not especially good for us? Perhaps we want to move interstate but we don't know anyone in our new town, and the prospect of striking out on our own is too lonely and scary. Or perhaps we think that retraining would give us more job options but we don't know anyone who can advise us on the best way to do this.

We face the prospect of leaving behind those who already care about us; and the people in the new network might not be receptive to an outsider, particularly one who doesn't know the rules.

This leads us to the big challenge we're trying to confront as a society and in the next few chapters: how to improve our social capital, or help others to do so, without spending the billions of dollars of the MTO programme. Can we build our social infrastructure without a handsome millionaire to support us? How do we find a Luke Danes to knock us into shape, or a Rory

Gilmore to give us something to aspire to? How do we find the courage to take a leap of faith into a new social situation and consequently risk the disruption of our existing capital? Can we help people to simulate the benefits of group membership without hundreds of years of history and rituals, or their forebears having had to fight a colonial oppressor? Let's find out.

10

Social Support

'A slayer with family and friends. That sure as hell wasn't in the brochure.'

Spike, *Buffy the Vampire Slayer*

A N IMPORTANT ASPECT of social capital is the support we can access through our network when we need it – for example, when we need advice, information or help getting out of trouble. In 2015, Michael was invited to a wedding – nothing unusual there; he was in his late twenties and getting married later that year himself. This was a bit different though. First, it was the wedding of one of his oldest friends, Pete, a Brit, who was marrying an American, Jamie and moving to Chicago. And second, the couple had asked Michael to register online as a valid minister and officiate the wedding. How could he refuse?

Unfortunately, Chicago is a long way away from Oxford, and so Michael, a post-doctoral student at this time, cashed in a favour from a professor friend and was duly invited to Indianapolis for two days of meetings and a seminar to talk about his research in charitable fundraising. Americans will tell you that Indianapolis is *very* close to Chicago. So, Michael could give his seminar on the Friday and travel up to Chicago on Saturday for the wedding. Easy.

The first lesson from this chapter, and possibly the most practical, is that you should always verify the distance between places yourself, rather than believing what people tell you. The second is that Americans, living as they do in a vast country with relatively few people in it, do not understand what 'very close' means. The journey from Indianapolis to Chicago by coach takes just over four hours, or roughly the amount of time it takes to get to Manchester from London. After receiving advice that he would 'definitely die' if he caught the Greyhound, Michael booked on to the 4 a.m. Megabus.

Michael's alarm went off at 2 a.m. – plenty of time to make it to the bus stop. On pulling back the curtains, however, he could see that it had snowed about six inches overnight. He checked Uber and couldn't get a car; reception couldn't get him a cab either. The sudden snow had closed the roads. There was only one thing for it: he walked, very slowly, the two miles from his hotel to the bus stop, arriving with ten minutes to spare.

Four a.m. came, but the bus didn't. Worry began to set in. It was incredibly cold,* still snowing, and without a minister the wedding wasn't happening. Michael called his friend Aisling, a person he knew he could always count on. Aisling very quickly identified that Michael's mood was somewhere between total panic and frozen to death, so she first calmed him down and then checked the internet. The bus wasn't running because of the snow. Aisling dispatched Michael back to his hotel (where it was at least warm) and looked for solutions. There was no way he could make it to the airport without a cab, but the Amtrak station was only a mile away and there was a train to Chicago leaving in twenty minutes.

---

* -9 degrees Celsius.

And so it came to pass that any local residents looking out of their window early on that February morning in Indianapolis would have seen a Brit in a bow tie and a fedora running down the middle of the street between banks of snow, with his suitcase held over his head. He *just* made it to the train and slumped into his seat with relief for the six-hour journey ahead of him, realizing only as he sorted himself out that below the snow on his hat was a half centimetre thick layer of ice.

After a few further minor mishaps, Michael made it to Chicago and officiated the wedding. Pete and Jamie are now living in Chicago, and Aisling is godmother to Michael's son.

Aisling forms a part of Michael's social capital, and highlights the important element of support you can access through your network to help you achieve your aims. Friendship is nice, and an important part of being alive, but to be a part of social capital friends have to helpful, whether that's a shoulder to cry on, a sofa to sleep on, or a frantic 4 a.m. phone call. If you have a person you can call to help get you out of Indianapolis at four in the morning, you probably have social capital.

But what if the people in your network are not very effective at helping you? For instance, maybe you have people who would want to help you get out of Indianapolis but wouldn't know where to start, or people who want to see you succeed academically but lack the knowledge or confidence to help you on your way. This might be classified as having low – but not no – social capital. You have social bonds – friends and family – but those bonds are not currently helping you achieve your aims.

One of the first people to explore this was Harvard professor Todd Rogers. Rogers theorized that when people who have some social capital are nonetheless struggling in an environment that requires that capital – say, education – it could be that the capital isn't being deployed in the right way, or isn't being deployed for that purpose.

In education, the first place to look is, of course, parents. From our own experiences in school, we know that there were some parents who were at every sports day, every football match, but never turned up to parents' evenings, and whose children struggled academically. These parents weren't ill-intentioned (hardly any parents are), and there's no real reason to doubt that they sincerely wanted their children to do well academically. But without communication between parents and children, and without parents knowing what their children were learning, and what they might need, they wouldn't be able to use the social capital within their existing networks well.

This is where Rogers comes in. He worked with Raj Chande, then a PhD student, and Simon Burgess, a professor of economics – both at Bristol University – and came up with an idea to get parents more involved in their kids' education.

Rogers had met Chande at a meeting in 10 Downing Street, the heart of the British government but, for all its power, not a place that could help put innovations in education into action. So they went to the Education Endowment Foundation (EEF). This was set up in 2011 by the UK's Department for Education and had £150 million at its disposal to improve educational outcomes for young people receiving free school meals in England. Under its chief executive, Sir Kevan Collins, the EEF had taken the unusual step of stipulating that anything they funded was not only evaluated but was *independently* evaluated using a randomized controlled trial – they have since then funded more than 150 large-scale trials. The evidence that this produces, and the way it has changed the centre of gravity in educational debate in Britain, means that it is difficult to think of a single institution that has done as much to change the face of education for the better in our lifetimes.

Most of the projects that the EEF have funded are expensive to run. They've found that Magic Breakfast, a charity that ensures young people get a good breakfast every morning in school, increases attainment by the equivalent of two months of schooling.[133] Another programme used additional philosophy lessons and activities for students to increase their maths grades by two months of schooling.[134] The Visible Classroom project, led by John Hattie at the University of Melbourne, has seen secondary school teachers in 100 schools wearing headsets for six weeks to record and measure their teaching styles.[135] Alongside these interventions, the EEF also commissioned evaluations that ultimately showed that a lot of things that people thought would improve students' grades – reduced class sizes, for example, or additional teaching assistants – actually had little impact and were quite bad value for money.[136]

As such, there was some initial scepticism about whether what Rogers, Burgess and Chande were proposing could make a difference. The idea attracted raised eyebrows not because it was so complicated but because it seemed so simple: to send parents text messages about what their students were studying, and about upcoming exams, in order that they could take a more active role in their children's learning.[137]

While the idea may have been simple, executing it was anything but. Chande and a team of four research assistants worked with the thirty-four pilot schools, collecting information about what should be sent out to parents, preparing the messages and, in many cases, manually implementing their sending and responding to any initial queries. A message might have said something like:

> Today, in Science, Mo learned about solids, liquids and gases. Ask him, which one is shaving foam?

Two years later, the results were in. The effects on the performance of students at sixteen years old were small but statistically significant – the equivalent of an extra one month of teaching, and all for just £5 per pupil. Speaking to Rogers about this, his frustration is clear: his research agenda, co-ordinated through the Student Social Support lab, is trying to strengthen social support for those people who need it most, and a broad-brush intervention across schools was always going to produce small effects because it would include many people who are already getting the support they need. So how can you try to find the people who most need help?

The answer to this question was clear in an American context. Rogers diverted his attention to community colleges and online or distance learning, where people didn't have the same social networks around them, and may have already left home.

Back in the UK, our thinking pointed in a similar direction. Much of adult education in the UK takes place in further education colleges; and prior to 2014, continuing or adult education was most of what these colleges did. Despite the revolution in empirical research in school-aged education, older years had been less well served (the EEF's mandate originally stopped at sixteen).

Part of the work of BIT's ASK research centre, which we first mentioned back in Chapter 8, was to fund the PhD of Bibi Groot, whose research was intended to explore ways of activating the social capital of adult learners. All this changed when, the year after ASK was set up, the government amended the rules about the GCSE exams students sit when they're sixteen.

If you do well in your GCSEs, you might have a better chance of getting into a good institution for your sixteen–eighteen education, which will in turn shape your path into the labour market or to university. Do OK, but not great, and you may find that your school won't let you take some subjects forward, limiting your career options later. Our research shows that when applying for the same job people with GCSEs are about twice as likely to get an interview as those who don't have any GCSEs.[138] In the past, students who hadn't succeeded in these exams couldn't study for more advanced academic qualifications, but could pursue vocational routes or enter into apprenticeships.

After the changes, young people who don't pass the maths or English exams need to re-sit them as part of any course of study. And being in some form of education is compulsory until age nineteen, which means students are effectively required to retake the GCSEs again – and again. The evidence, sadly, is that most students who failed the first time will turn nineteen before they pass. This shouldn't be a surprise – if you don't pass first go, you then find yourself in a college with typically larger class sizes, fewer contact hours and less funding per student. Psychologically, the price of failing is also high: research on planning and goal-setting shows that initial failure can be highly off-putting to future attempts – so that failing something the first time makes it more likely you'll fail the second time.

It's no shock then that these young people often feel isolated, and like they don't belong. Many of us would fall back on our social support networks in such difficult times, and rely on our parents to support us. However, often students' parents, and those in their networks, may care about them and want to help, but, as we've seen above, the students might not know how to activate that social capital effectively.

This is where Groot stepped in. At the beginning of the school year, she got students to complete an online form nominating a 'study supporter' – someone who cared about their learning. These didn't have to be parents (although many of them were) – it could be an uncle or aunt, a friend, a cousin, a girlfriend,* or even a social worker. As well as basic information, like their first name, Groot asked students to provide the supporter's mobile

---

* This isn't a good idea – the romantic relationships of sixteen-year-olds are intense but, sadly, often brief.

number. Then, throughout the year, the supporters were sent messages that aimed to act as conversation starters to help them talk about what the young people were studying. For example:

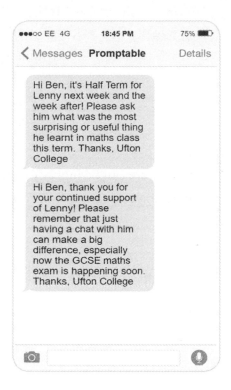

The intervention was very light – thirty-five messages over the course of the year – but it was impactful, and managed to increase pass rates by 27 per cent. The effects were biggest for boys, who started with lower pass rates than girls. These results were replicated the following year. Alongside this, Groot was interviewing students to find out how the programme was working. The feedback was positive:

I think it was three weeks ago or something, because when we had an exam three weeks ago, and then I was sleeping and he called me up, and then he was like you have an exam and I was like oh f**k and I had to run for it. Andrew,* student

Yeah, I do love it, because no matter what she will support me and she help me like her best, so it takes a lot of weight off me. Yvonne,† student

Some students, like Andrew, reported that the support worked for them because the supporters could give them prompts where they hadn't had any before. Other students, like Yvonne, talked about the emotional benefits of the supporter – someone they already knew taking an interest in their studies. Quickly a coherent pattern in the data emerged, of people's existing capital being activated in new directions.

We can all think of dozens of situations in our lives when a bit of extra support might come in handy – when we've just been diagnosed with a disease, when we're starting a new job or coming up for promotion. How broad could the application of this work be? At the same time, the process is labour intensive. Running Chande's study took four research assistants, and setting up and managing Study Supporter took time and, of course, money.

On the other side of the Atlantic, Rogers knew this, and worked with Johannes Demarzi to set up a new social enterprise – *In Class Today*, which works with school districts across the US to reduce chronic absenteeism by getting these interventions to a much wider group of students. In the UK, Groot took a different tack, helping found the tech start-up Promptable. Promptable takes the

---

* Not his real name.
† Not her real name.

interventions based on social support and puts it to use in schools, colleges and the corporate world.

We saw in Chapter 6 how Lendlease and the Movember Foundation used competition and social comparison to get their staff to be more active, but what about taking a more supportive approach? Could companies help to improve the fitness of their employees by adding 'habit helpers' to corporate wellness programmes? This would let staff sign up with their wearable device to have information sent to a nominated friend – nothing too invasive, but enough to give them a nudge out the door for a run on those cold winter mornings. If integrated in the workplace, where increasingly our colleagues are also our friends, it could suggest activities your habit helper and you could do together – like going for a walk, or a quick game of Quidditch.* It could also let them know about any goals you set and how you're getting on, giving you someone in your corner on a rainy morning when you don't want to leave the house.†

If we can increase grades, and physical activity, what about tackling harder problems such as Type 2 diabetes? Emerging later in life than Type 1 diabetes and often arising from an unhealthy lifestyle, Type 2 is on the rise in the developed world. In the UK the rate of Type 2 diabetes has more than doubled in the last twenty years – from 1.4 million in 1996 to 3.5 million in 2016.[139] The picture in the US is much the same, with rates rising from 5.5 per cent in 1994 to 9.3 per cent in 2012, and the Centers for Disease Control (CDC) is forecasting that a third of the population might

---

* You might laugh, but Oxford has a Quidditch league that Michael walks past (but ardently does not participate in) on Saturday mornings: see http://www.ouqc.uk
† Oxford also has a lot of those.

have diabetes by 2050.[140] Even reducing that to 49 per cent could save 38,000 lives globally each year.[141]

Diabetes and other 'lifestyle diseases' pose a significant challenge to the health, wellbeing and productivity of the world's population, especially when we consider that in the future, with that population ageing, there will be more people in the workforce with health conditions they need to manage. With businesses losing valuable time to sickness like this, integrating with corporate wellness makes a lot of sense.

A diagnosis like diabetes (or pre-diabetes) is a shock, but the good news is that for many people lifestyle changes such as a healthier diet, more exercise and quitting smoking can reverse the onset of the condition or at least make it manageable.[142] Despite this, in the majority of cases pre-diabetes progresses to diabetes and people struggle to regulate their condition. Added to this, the largest group of people who develop diabetes are male and from lower-income backgrounds – exactly the same group that benefited most from the Study Supporter intervention in schools, in part because they were the least likely to make use of their own social capital.

We think that health management is the next frontier for social support. Middle-aged men, the group most affected by diabetes, have families, children, friends, colleagues – they know how they'd answer the 'Indianapolis question' – but they don't pick up the phone when they get a diagnosis like this and need to make major changes to their lives: when they could really use some support. But, like parents who may not know how best to help their teenagers with maths – or that their teenager might welcome some help – we may not know how to help someone managing a health condition. A programme in a similar vein to

Study Supporter might work here, and there's a strong case for employers investing in this as part of their wellness programmes. But if you're managing a condition like diabetes, think about who could support you and reach out to ask them. You might be surprised by how much people want to help.

We can also consider other ways that we can help staff make more use of their networks. For instance, we know that starting a new job can be stressful, especially for recent graduates. Support from friends and family is often an important element of a successful transition into the workforce. Although it may not be appropriate for employers to text your parents when you have a performance appraisal coming up, employers could develop advice on how to mobilize support from our networks. Talking to others about something that's stressing you out at work comes more naturally to some people – but we could encourage new employees to think about who they would like to support them, and to ask that person to be there for them (we could even draw on the insights from Part 1, about how we join new social groups and how important they are to make this conversation more likely to happen). Likewise, employers could encourage employees to bring people who support them to after-work drinks sometimes – the conversation would be 'There's free drinks and food', but the benefit would be that the supporter would get to know the work environment and be better able to support the employee.

For many organizations, leveraging social support in and around the workplace feels like a natural extension of a lot of the work that already goes on building teams and encouraging a corporate culture of support. Team hikes, yoga, playing volleyball or eating lunch (or indeed, going to the pub) together are all symptoms and causes of people having friends at work, something that research by the polling company Gallup suggests is an important part of employee wellbeing and retention. If employers add a layer of structure around the existing social environment, particularly geared towards things that they know employees struggle with, they might be surprised by the scale of the results they see.

In this chapter we've looked at a fundamental element of social capital: who in your network can help you achieve your goals, be they in education or work, health or getting you out of a sticky situation when you're overseas. For many people, the social support they can access is greater than they realize: they just need to know how to mobilize it. However, for others, the level and type of social support they can access is fundamentally limited by who's in their network. The people they know and rely on may not be able to support them if their life takes them in a very different direction. In these cases, we need to think about how people build new networks in new places, which is the focus of the next chapter.

11

Social Bridging

'There's something beautiful about finding one's innermost thoughts in another.'

Olive Schreiner

STARTING IN A new place is tough – whether it's a new town, a new job or a new school. Entering an alien environment by yourself, you can very quickly become lost. If you're lucky, you'll find someone to guide you through this treacherous new environment – a Sam to your Frodo, so you don't have to trek to Mordor alone.*

For Susannah, it wasn't so much Mordor as Canberra – although many Australians will tell you there isn't much to choose between them. Moving cities in Australia isn't trivial: it is almost always necessary to fly between them, which is expensive, and Susannah had never really considered living in Canberra until the day she found herself, after two years working in Brisbane, accepting a position in the Department of the Prime Minister and Cabinet.

The division was expanding, and so they had hired quite a

---

* Or Bilbo, if you like your adventures less epic or your movies more drawn-out.

few people who were all starting at the same time. People tend to move to Canberra as part of graduate cohorts for the various departments, so moving later than that, as Susannah was about to, was quite intimidating.

However, the division organized an away day a couple of months before, which the new starters were all able to join. It was a chance to not only meet the division, but also the other new starters, and to learn a bit about who she'd be working with.

Despite having developed various game plans for how she was going to impress all these public service high-flyers with her knowledge, skills and confidence, Susannah was extremely nervous: after all, most people in the room were going to know each other, and what if she didn't get along with any of the other new starters?

However, when she walked into the room, she saw a familiar face: one of the new starters was Tess, with whom Susannah had become friends on a bus tour of Spain four years previously, but lost touch. Tess was in a very similar situation, moving from Sydney to Canberra, and from state to federal government, and the power of a familiar face was such that Susannah didn't feel so alone. She was able to get to know her new colleagues, confident that there was already one person she was going to be working with that she knew and liked.

Tess and Susannah were able to commiserate about how the ways of the Canberra public service were different to what they were used to: a valuable sanity check in a new environment. The social bridge formed by knowing Tess and the other new starters from that first away day helped Susannah to get through the various tribulations of uprooting her life and trying to settle somewhere new.

One of the other new starters, Steph, also introduced the Japanese concept of *douki* to the group. Japanese firms tend to hire people in large rounds, and the people in these rounds are *douki*, which translates to 'same group'. Because Japanese companies tend to hire people expecting that they will be there for their whole career, your *douki* are like comrades, or siblings – you're expected to look out for each other as you progress together through the organization. The *douki* group met regularly for breakfast while all of them lived in Canberra, sharing news and offering each other support.

It was also links through PM&C that ultimately inspired Susannah to move to London, and through whom she met Gabrielle, another Brisbanite-turned-Canberran who was also moving to London, and who would become her first London friend.

We've seen in previous chapters that our instinct to respond to a social situation is strong – we react to social norms even when they're implicit, forming social groups and working hard to live up to their ideals. When we see a role model, someone like us who is thriving, we aspire to be like them (something we'll look at more in Chapter 12). When we find ourselves in a new environment without social support or a role model, we reach out and start forming new links with those around us – or making friends, as most people call it.

The relief of having a friend in a new environment is huge. Without it, you can feel like you're in freefall. For almost all of us, the freefall stage is short-lived, but those first few freefalling weeks in a new job or a new city can be exhausting and keep us from being happy and therefore also from performing at our best. We personally know of two colleagues who moved to London from America, and the difference in their situations highlights the power of this connection.

One colleague had friends and family already in town, while the other was much more isolated. A year on, both have thriving social networks and are, in fact, close friends with each other. But go back six months, and the colleague who had a social network on arrival was living in a house she was happy with and was being recommended for promotion. The other was still trying out different living arrangements and had struggled with managing her workload – in other words, she was still freefalling.

BIT's collaboration with King's College London (see Chapter 4) explored questions around how people adjust to new environments through a six-wave panel study of 750 first-year students, and through a series of randomized control trials. One of the things we particularly wanted to explore was students' feelings of connectedness to – and identification with – various people in the institution. We asked them some questions to gauge the extent to which they felt similar to others around them, and satisfied with their interactions with peers and staff. We asked first in November of their first year, and then again in the following July, after they'd got their exam results.

We saw significant differences in the degrees to which various students felt satisfied with their peer groups. In particular, we saw a small but persistent difference overall between students from low-income backgrounds and those from more traditionally university-bound families. When we controlled for gender, ethnicity and faculty, we saw that a great deal of this was driven by black students and male students feeling less connected to their peers. Even more interestingly, students who were more satisfied with their peer groups at the beginning of the year also did better in their exams.

These findings inspired us to explore ways we could help

students who might be wondering whether they fit in with their peers to interpret ambiguous cues more positively through correcting their perceptions of the social norms. It also got us thinking about how we could encourage students to build stronger, more satisfying friendship networks.

One excellent way to make friends at university is to join a student society. Membership of student societies, such as sports clubs or cultural groups, is associated with a range of benefits, including better grades, higher wellbeing and better graduate outcomes. However, students from low-income backgrounds are less likely to join student societies, because they feel like it's beside the point of university or because they have other work and family commitments.

We wanted to encourage students to go to the Student Union welcome fair and consider joining societies, so we designed two sets of text messages with this end in mind. In one group, we aimed to address the potential perception that student societies were an 'optional extra' by telling students that:

Students who join societies and clubs get better grades, are happier and more employable.

In the other group, we informed students that:

The welcome fair is the best opportunity to meet societies and sports clubs. It's a great way to meet likeminded new people.

We also had a control group who weren't texted. We saw that around 60 per cent of students in the control group attended the welcome fair.

Students who were texted were significantly more likely to attend; in particular, students who received the friendship message. Most interestingly, we saw that low-income students were more likely to attend if they received the friendship SMS than the employability SMS – fewer low-income students receiving the employability message attended the welcome fair than did from the control group, although this was not statistically significant. Students who weren't from low-income backgrounds, however, responded strongly and positively to both messages. So, what does this tell us?

Well, it flows against conventional wisdom, which is that low-income students are more instrumentally motivated about university. If this were the case, the employability message should have increased their interest in signing up to societies, since that was linked to better grades and better job outcomes. Instead, we see a universal responsiveness to the friendship message, and particularly among groups who might be more likely to worry about fitting in at university.

So we can encourage students to engage with opportunities to make friends once they turn up to university, but what about situations when they might not even turn up for fear of not fitting in and finding friends?

A promising solution came from research carried out by Janna Ter Meer, the head of research at the online research start-up Predictiv, and Silvia Saccardo from Carnegie Mellon. Ter Meer and Saccardo carried out a study to try to increase the rate at which parents of young children turned up to classes held by government-funded centres to support families – a study also undertaken as part of the ASK research centre, like the Transport for London research in Chapter 8, and the Study Supporter project in Chapter 10. In this study, they tested the effect of incentives – parents were paid if they turned up to 80 per cent of the classes – and found that it increased attendance by 50 per cent.

This finding is useful for getting people to turn up to class, but is straight out of a traditional economics textbook: people respond to incentives. The other thing Ter Meer and Saccardo tested was a 'buddy incentive'. When people register for the class, they're also assigned a buddy – someone else taking the same course as them. This person is a total stranger, and they won't meet until the first class, but they're given a joint incentive: if they both turn up to class 80 per cent of the time, they'll get the incentive; but if either one of them doesn't make that goal, neither of them gets any money. This forces people together, and creates from scratch the kind of social capital that Groot relied on for her interventions. If Susannah knows that her getting paid depends on Michael turning up as much as it depends on her doing so, she's more likely to text him the night before – 'Are you going to class tomorrow? Need a lift?' – making them both more likely to make it to class. And this is exactly what Ter Meer and Saccardo found: by creating a social connection that wouldn't have been there before, the buddy incentive increased class attendance by 72 per cent.

This finding was exciting – it seemed like the combination of random pairing with a stranger, a common cause and a small amount of money could create a useful form of social capital.

The chance to try out this approach again came as part of a project with the National Citizen Service (NCS). The NCS programme brings together about 100,000 young people a year to take part in fun outdoor activities and social-action projects to help improve the world or their local community. Repeated evaluations show that it boosts social trust, confidence and openness to other cultures and ideas among participants; and, because it's heavily subsidized by the UK government, there are few barriers to attending.

Nonetheless, about 20 per cent of young people who sign up (register for a place and pay £50) don't actually attend the programme. This presents the programme with a quandary. The evidence from the independent evaluation of NCS suggests that the people who benefit the most from it are the people who are hardest to get to show up. The programme boosts social capital and social trust for young people, and tens of thousands aren't showing up – seemingly because they lack social capital. It would be ironic if it weren't so important. 'It's frustrating,' Michael Lynas, the CEO of NCS, says. 'The programme has been rigorously evaluated, and we know it makes people more confident, helps them make friends – and we can't get people on to it because they lack confidence. It's like … just come on the programme and then you'll want to go on the programme!'

The task of increasing NCS's turn-up rates fell to Clare Delargy, Head of Social Action at BIT. She looked at the problem at hand. As Lynas says, the challenge in getting people to turn up to a programme where they'll make friends is that they don't have any friends before they arrive. Once they arrive, though, they do a pretty good job of making friends – so why not bring that experience forward?

Delargy and her colleagues developed Networky. Networky's algorithm takes the list of people who have signed up to NCS and puts them into pairs, based on a few criteria. Everyone is paired with someone the same age as them but who attends a different school and is going to NCS at the same time in the same place (the programme runs nationally, with different 'waves' starting each week in the summer and at dozens of locations). It then sends each member of the pair a text message each week – first introducing them then providing conversational prompts like those shown below.

When people click on the links in the text, they are taken to a secure site where they can message their buddy. The communication is restricted – it prevents the participants from swearing, or sharing phone numbers or email addresses, but lets them talk about whatever else they want:[143] their exams, their hopes for the future or of course NCS.

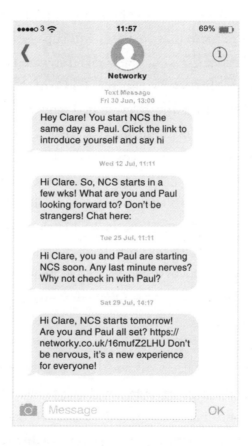

As well as testing Networky, Delargy worked with Ter Meer and Saccardo on an incentivized version of Networky, where the pairs would receive a small incentive (Amazon vouchers) if both of them turned up but nothing if either of them failed to do so. The participants were paired four weeks before they were due to attend NCS, and thousands of messages passed between participants over the course of that time.

When the final analysis was completed, the results were surprising: the platform was working, with both groups that used Networky about a third less likely to drop out before the programme started. However, the financial incentives didn't have an additional impact – in, fact, the effect of Networky plus the financial incentives was smaller than the effect of Networky itself – strongly suggesting that the impact was from creating new social ties and not in the financial incentive.

When you dig into the data, the picture gets even more interesting. Delargy had hypothesized beforehand that people could find comfort in being paired with a buddy like themselves – of the same ethnicity or religion, perhaps – and that this might make them more likely to show up. As it turns out, the *opposite* was true – people were most likely to turn up when they were buddied up with someone who was *different* to them. So, someone from a lower-income background was most likely to attend if their buddy was someone from a more affluent background, and young people from ethnic minorities were most likely to show up if their buddy was white. It's as if being able to encounter someone socially distant, and close that gap early, made people more relaxed about the whole programme, and more likely to get on the bus. Once at NCS, people who'd had a buddy before attending reported higher levels of satisfaction and enjoyment of their time there than those who hadn't. After two successful studies, the programme was taken to scale in the summer of 2018, and tens of thousands of young people were formed into pairs to communicate with each other.

As all this was being decided, late in 2017, and with this initial success behind her, Delargy started building her own team to handle a growing workload. After a long recruitment process, she had someone she wanted to appoint – let's call her Delilah. She came with excellent references and a superb CV, having completed a PhD and postdoctoral studies at top universities. Happy with the appointment, Delilah's start date was scheduled for the team's away day – to give her a chance to meet the team and ease into a new working environment during a day that combined training with some fun activities.

At 3 p.m. the day before, Delilah emailed the human resources department to say that she wouldn't be taking up the job after all. Since accepting the job, she'd been thinking about what it meant to leave academic life behind and enter the very different world of consulting, and had decided to stay where she was.

Delilah's decision had obviously been a tough one for her to make. She'd spoken with enthusiasm about the new job throughout the interview process, but ultimately that leap into the unknown was just too much for her. As we've seen elsewhere in this book, entering an environment where you don't have any social connections is difficult, and something that most people go out of their way to avoid. Anyone who's hired lots of people will be familiar with the annoyance of your preferred candidate turning you down for another job – sometimes (surprisingly often) the job they already have.

For Delargy, though, this was doubly frustrating – and ironic. She'd been hiring Delilah, in part, to work on the Networky project, helping people do new things by building their social network before they arrived. And Delilah hadn't turned up because she felt unable to leave her old job, with a strong social network, to move into a very new and different one where she didn't yet have a network.

Inspired by this setback in her own team, Delargy spoke to her HR department about deploying Networky for a new purpose: to help people before they start work.

The process is simple. If you're offered a job at a company, let's say the Behavioural Insights Team, you're assigned a buddy as soon as you accept the offer – usually someone at the same position (or maybe a bit higher) in the hierarchy as you'll be, and in the same team you'll be joining.

Over the course of the four weeks before you join the company, you'll each be sent a series of text messages – much like the ones sent to the NCS participants – prompting discussion between you and your buddy, as shown below.

In a small company, social linking into the organization in this way can help develop mentoring relationships early on and make people feel more at home.

In larger organizations, this kind of bridging capital might not be as easy to create, especially if there's a larger cohort of people starting at the same time – for example as part of a graduate scheme. In the last chapter we considered how we could help people transition into the workforce by mobilizing their existing networks, but a more fruitful approach may actually be to help them build new ones.

The graduate scheme at Teach First, which takes high-achieving graduates and places them into schools, typically in deprived areas, working as teachers after a short training course, takes on 1,750 graduates a year and is the largest graduate programme in the UK.[144] Other large employers, like PricewaterhouseCoopers or KPMG, take about 1,200, and the civil service takes about 1,000. In the US, accounting firm Ernst & Young hires 5,000 graduates a year. Co-ordinating mentors for all of them might well

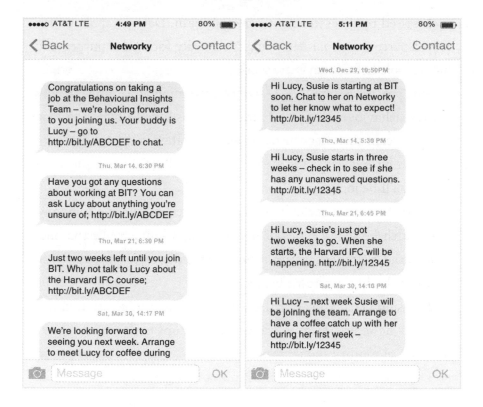

be impossible, particularly in industries where attrition is high – perhaps as much as 50 per cent in the first year. If most people don't make it to the second year, you won't have enough survivors to be mentors for the next cohort and you might even have the kind of survivorship bias that we see in the 'hazing', or initiation that takes place when people join some college fraternities in the US. People know that it's wrong, but still visit the same violence on the next generation that they themselves received. The reason? If I had to go through something, even if it was terrible, so should the next guy – I don't want them having an easy ride.

By contrast, your own peers coming into a graduate training programme can be either your best friends or your worst enemies.

If you're introduced to them only when you start in a competitive environment, where impressing the bosses is what might make the difference between surviving that first year or not, you might be less open to making new friends. If, however, you've already exchanged a few messages and bonded a little before you first meet it could be harder to turn on each other in a high-pressure environment.

Organizations function more smoothly and more effectively when information and ideas can freely flow and trust is higher – something that we'll come on to in more detail in Chapter 13. When we set up graduate schemes as competitive, winners-take-all tournaments with high dropout rates, our instincts tell us that we're creating an environment where, through survival of the fittest, the best ideas will be generated. The evidence suggests not only that this needs rethinking, but also that an intervention to create a social bridge between groups might be part of the solution.

In this chapter we've looked at ways to help people build social capital in new spheres, by getting a head start on making connections before they arrive. Meeting a large number of people simultaneously can be overwhelming, and we've seen that having the opportunity to 'dip your toe' into the waters of a new environment by meeting a couple of people first helps you stick with your intention to turn up, and results in a more enjoyable experience.

If social bridging helps build capital, it may not be enough by itself to get us started by building a bridge between our current networks and new ones, especially when those new networks are remote. Showing that the alien worlds of other networks are, in fact, Earth after all, is the topic of the next chapter.

12

Role Models

'To boldly go where no one has gone before.'

Zefram Cochrane, *Star Trek*

'If I have seen further, it is by standing on the shoulders of giants.'

Sir Isaac Newton

IT'S 21 AUGUST 2003, in the small village of Alveston, just outside Bristol, England. At the local comprehensive school, students are turning up despite it being the middle of the school holidays. The local press have a reporter on the ground. It is GCSE results day.

It's a big day, obsessed over in commentary pieces about the state of the nation. If grades go up, exams must be getting easier. If grades go down, children must be getting dumber. Back in 2003, you could leave school at sixteen – for some people, the grades they got that day would determine if they continued in education at all, and for some they would be the only qualifications that they'd be taking into the job market.

On this particular day, we're interested in two students. Both are about the same height with the same hair colour. Their families are similar in terms of income, and they live in the same area. They go to the school, pick up their envelopes from the school library, and slink off to open them in private before reporting back to their families. Both get the same mix of pretty good results. At this stage they are, statistically speaking, close to identical on the things we'd naturally think to look at when comparing two young people's educational outcomes.

Immediately after this moment, their circumstances diverge. One of them – let's call him Nick – leaves school that day never to return, following in his father's footsteps to pursue a career that requires no additional qualifications. The other stays at school, gets average grades at A levels (the exams taken in the UK at eighteen), and goes on to an average university. Fourteen years later, one of them has found the sector he followed his father into ravaged by a changing world, and the other is writing this book.

So, how do two people who seem so similar end up on such different paths? Personality, motivation and family influences play a part.

What made the difference in Michael and Nick's case? The answer might lie in a GCSE business studies class. Both took the class, and both got the same grades. The difference, though, is that Nick didn't turn up to class very often, for one reason or another. The teacher of this class was a man called Steve Clark. Mr Clark was a teacher of the 'tell a lot of stories that are related to the subject matter and hope that it sticks' type, and so students (those who turned up to class, at least) heard all about his life as an essential part of the learning process. We heard about his daughter, who is about the same age as us, and we heard about his four endowment mortgages, one of which was necessary because his roof had fallen in. Most importantly, we heard about his time at Cambridge University, in the voice of Mr Clark – who sounded, like the rest of us, like he lived in the

West Country, and not like the plummy-voiced people we would naturally associate with a university like Cambridge. Mr Clark's stories made university, and elite university in particular, feel like an attainable goal, and one that would be enjoyable enough to be worth attaining. Michael, yes, turned up at school more than Nick, but without Mr Clark's influence, Michael would have done the same as Nick had, and wouldn't have seriously considered university. Michael has still, fifteen years later, not made it to Cambridge, but that was the moment that the germ of an idea started for him – while Nick was cutting class.

Role models can influence us regardless of whether they are people we know, if they are prominent and aspirational. Jennifer Aniston's haircut in the first few seasons of *Friends* became so popular it is still known as the 'Rachel'; and similarly it may be no coincidence that Michael's trademark look came about just as Matt Smith first took to the TARDIS in *Doctor Who*. Most of us can think of someone we looked up to as a child (or adult) and who inspired some of our life decisions.

The two quotes at the beginning of the chapter highlight an essential conflict in the way we think about how change happens. Whether it is technological innovation, social progress or major life events, as Isaac Newton acknowledged, much progress is the result of marginal changes to what came before – standing on the shoulder of giants. If we're to boldly go where nobody (in our family) has gone before, it's helpful for most of us to know that it's possible, and that someone like us has done something like it before. Yet our popular narrative about success is a kind of 'big bang' – about the kid who rises from the very bottom to the very top in a single generation. Those people certainly do exist, but if we're looking for people who are going to not just rise but impact the world this might be unrealistic and actively unhelpful.

Continuing in education makes total sense in a selfish world. Research by Lindsey Macmillan from University College London's Institute of Education, and Paul Gregg at the University of Bath, shows that half of all social immobility[145] is driven by education. As we've mentioned, in the UK people who go to university earn on average £200,000 more over their lifetime than people who don't, and people who go to selective universities earn even more. Anyone thinking about future earnings alone would naturally stay in education well after sixteen.[146] University-qualified professions also tend, on the whole, to be more resilient to globalization and technological change, and people with degrees tend to have less trouble changing sectors, whereas many traditional working-class occupations are in decline.

But stories like Nick's at the start of this chapter can be found across Britain – and this problem is particularly the case among Britain's white working class. In the Longitudinal Study of Young People in England, hundreds of young people are followed through their lives and asked questions about, among other things, their attitudes to education.

In the survey, 26 per cent of all white students indicated that 'People like me do not go to university' – higher than any other ethnic group. The problem is starker for boys than for girls – 30 per cent compared to 21 per cent, and this figure gets worse when you look at some of the other questions.

Among white boys, 58 per cent said that they were either unlikely, or very unlikely, to apply to university compared to 46 per cent for white girls, 26 per cent for black Caribbean students, and 6 per cent for black african students, who reported the highest anticipated likelihood of attending university. When you account for the fact that 97 per cent of students at the mostly white private school Eton College attend university – and 29 per cent attend the elite universities of Oxford and Cambridge[147] – we see a heavily bifurcated white population: at one end are the elite, with a likelihood of going to university nearing 100 per cent; and at the other the working class, with a likelihood close to 0 per cent.

The problem is particularly acute in rural areas, and particularly those areas where there are no universities. One such area is the county of Somerset, in the south-west of the UK. Somerset is a large county but sparsely populated, with no cities.[148] The county doesn't score highly on educational aspiration – it's in the bottom 10 per cent of counties for university attendance, and in the bottom 15 per cent for attending selective Russell Group[149] universities.[150]

Tackling this lack of educational aspiration was one of the priorities for the Somerset Challenge – an umbrella group of the county's secondary schools, set up in 2013 to help improve education across the county through collaboration.[151]

The Behavioural Insights Team first met with Simon Faull, the director of the Somerset Challenge, in January 2014, shortly after the Challenge had begun. Over the course of the initial hour-long conversation, the possibility of collaboration became apparent.

Faull, a former teacher and now senior figure in the local government of Somerset, had managed the impressive feat of convincing the heads of more than thirty schools to contribute to a pooled budget to help them tackle their shared challenges, and was now in desperate need of new ideas – Somerset schools had already tried what they could think of, and something different was, in Faull's view, the only way to make progress.

At the same time, we'd been thinking a lot about how

behavioural science could tackle this very issue. Inspired by a paper by Jake Anders at University College London's Institute of Education, which showed that the lack of people from low-income families in elite universities could be explained in part by people not applying to those universities, this felt like a perfect area for a nudge. Add the fact that Michael was born in Weston-Super-Mare, in North Somerset, and this became a dream project.

The clear message from Anders' research was that there was a crop of young people from low-income families who had the right grades to go to good universities but who weren't applying, when their richer peers with the same (or worse) grades were. The hard work of addressing educational inequality was already done here. These young people had already studied hard and struggled against the odds to get great grades, and were stopping short, just before applying to university. Dilip Soman, a professor of marketing at the Rotman school at the University of Toronto, calls this a 'last mile'[152] problem – the technical, hard work has been done, and we enter the domain of psychology: how do we get people to fill in that application form?

To answer this a small team was deployed to conduct interviews with students and their teachers in Somerset over the course of a week. Two themes emerged from these interviews. The first was the idea of cost: the government had recently increased tuition fees to £9,000 per year and this was preventing people from applying.

This was the topic of some debate in the converted barn the team was living in for the week. The cost of going to university – tuition fees, living expenses and how much you earn after university (which would either make those costs worth it, or not), was a structural factor, not something that could be nudged.

But university in the UK is, from an end-user perspective, free at the point of use – nobody, from Prince Harry down to the lowliest commoner, pays their tuition fees on arrival; and everyone is eligible for financial support in the form of student loans, with additional grants available for people whose parents don't earn much money. Unlike in the US, student loans don't need to be paid back until people are earning money, and at the time of our work the changes to that tuition-fee threshold had also increased the repayment threshold. Weirdly, this meant that for most new graduates, the amount they were paying back on their student loans was actually less than it would have been had fees been lower.[153] Maybe, went the argument, people were put off by the perception of tuition fees, and if we set them right, they'd go?

The second theme that emerged was about the lack of role models. Most students were from families where nobody had been to university before, and which had been living in Somerset for generations. The popular perception of a university student, and especially an elite university student, was someone posh, someone Etonian, like the prime minister at the time, David Cameron, or the chancellor, George Osborne[154] – certainly someone who belonged to none of the social groups that these students identified with. Of course, as was pointed out to the team in the debrief with teachers at the end of the week, all of their teachers had been to university, and many of them to good ones. Weren't the teachers themselves inspiring enough? It seemed not.

The information-barrier problem seemed an obvious one to try to overcome first – we just had to tell everyone about the real costs and benefits of university. We quickly put together two sets of postcards – one for young people themselves, and one for their parents. Each set of three cards contained information on salary, financial support and loan repayment:

If you go to university, you're likely to earn £200,000 more over your lifetime.	You don't pay any tuition fees until you are earning more than £21,000 per year.	Parents don't earn that much? Your tuition fees can be halved. You can also get over £3,000 a year that you don't pay back.

Our attention then turned to how we could solve the problem of the lack of role models, and settled on a talk from someone from the same area of the country, from a similar background as the students, who had gone to university and enjoyed it. After calling everyone we could think of, it was pointed out that a member of our own team was from that part of the world, and had a very similar story to tell – in fact, we already told it here at the start of this chapter. In the most awkward meeting Michael can remember, he found himself put forward not as a behavioural scientist trying to design an intervention to increase access to university, but as the intervention itself.

We randomly selected where the talks would be given, and to which year groups within a school. We also distributed the informational cards at random – some tutor groups were chosen to receive them, and some weren't, while some parents were selected to get them and others weren't.

A few months later, young people from all the different groups were surveyed and asked their feelings about going to university: how interested were they in going, and how likely did they think they were to go?

The data that came back was surprising. When a student's parents were sent cards that gave them better information about the university fees system, it didn't do anything at all – the student didn't have better information about fees, or the financial return to going to university, and certainly didn't consider themselves more likely to go.

The other two interventions fared better to begin with – students who received the cards or who received the talk from Michael were more likely to answer factual questions correctly – multiple-choice questions like 'How much extra are you likely to earn if you go to university?' – which suggests that the information was getting across, and that students were remembering it, even months later.

At this point, however, the two stories diverged. Students who received the cards actually said they were significantly *less* likely to attend university than students who hadn't received the cards – even though they knew that it would make them financially better off. On the other hand, students who received the talk said they were significantly *more* likely to go to university, compared to the group that didn't receive cards or a talk. We found similar results when we asked all the students about their level of interest in going to university, which gives us a better measure of motivation as it doesn't make students consider their grades.

We'd found that the role-model intervention works – we can inspire people by showing them someone who had been where they are and had now moved on. But why did it work? As well as the questions about money, and people's feelings about university, we asked them some more emotive, social questions.

The cards given to students had increased students' knowledge of the financial considerations of attending university, but they hadn't changed their beliefs about the more social side of things. Students who received the talk, however, were significantly *more* likely to think that people who attend university would meet interesting people, and spent more time with their friends, and were less likely to agree that university wasn't for 'people like them' – and these questions were the most predictive of not attending university.

We came away from the study[155] both pleased and frustrated.

Role models were effective at boosting aspirations, and we had a good idea of how they worked. The financial side of university was obviously important, but it wasn't enough without that social impetus to go, that sense that 'people like you' could do it. On the other hand, the intervention wasn't easily scalable – it's one thing to drive around Somerset for a week giving talks, but turning that into a scalable programme would be a massive undertaking.

Conveniently, the wheels were already in motion for a larger-scale, lighter-touch version of the same intervention: a national campaign that aimed to get young people to apply to more selective universities, once again using role models. The campaign was devised by Michael, Raj Chande, developer of the parent-texting intervention we saw in Chapter 10 and now head of education at BIT, and Tim Leunig, then a special advisor at the Department for Education and later the chief economist there.

Students who were in the top 20 per cent nationally in their GCSE results, and who attended schools where the majority of students who apply to university apply to the one closest to the school (which is used as a proxy for low aspiration), were written to by two young people who had selected to be role models. Both role models were students at the University of Bristol who had come from similar situations to the students they were writing to. One of them, Ben, wrote a letter (see opposite), which was sent in an official-looking envelope, and on Department for Education headed paper, aimed to emphasize not only that university could be cheaper than the students might have thought but also that their choice of university mattered.

The second student, Rachel, aimed to emphasize the same important facts, but her letter (on page 224) was sent to students' home addresses, in the hope that they would be more likely to discuss it with their parents.

Department for Education

Please send any queries to:
Department for Education
Sanctuary Buildings
Great Smith Street
London
SW1P 3BT
www.education.gov.uk/help/contactus/dfe

[full name]
[House number]
[Street]
[Town / City]
[Postcode]

A message from Ben Cole, currently studying at University of Bristol

Dear [firstname]

Congratulations on your outstanding GCSE results! Your results place you in the top few percent of students in the country.

Back in 2009, I was in exactly the same position as you. I had good GCSE grades but I didn't know what to do next. I decided to apply to university and after doing some research and attending a few open days I came to realise that people with grades like you and me are in high demand from very prestigious universities.

Choosing the right university for you is an important decision, as every university will offer a different experience. For example a university may be based in a city or on a campus, or offer more in the way of sports or the arts. Which? Magazine and the National Union of Students have created a website to give you honest advice about different places you could choose. If I could give you any advice it would be to think long term – the reality is that employers care about which university you attend.

A very common mistake that people make when choosing their university is thinking that more prestigious universities are more expensive. This is not always the case, as these universities often have larger grants (money you are given and don't have to pay back) and government loans are more generous if you choose to live away from home. Remember, university should be seen as an investment in your future rather than a short term cost, so you should consider a wide range of options before making any decisions.

Your grades mean that you have a bright future ahead of you. However, I urge you to consider all your options as with grades such as yours you may have even more options than you realise.

Yours sincerely,

Research has shown that providing young people with better information on the costs and benefits of attending different universities helps them make better decisions about their future. The Department for Education has arranged for pupils that have performed very well in their GCSEs to receive letters from a current university student explaining how to find out more.

**Department
for Education**

Please send any queries to:
Department for Education
Sanctuary Buildings
Great Smith Street
London
SW1P 3BT
www.education.gov.uk/help/contactus/dfe

[full name]
[House number]
[Street]
[Town / City]
[Postcode]

A message from Rachel Prescott, currently studying at University of Bristol

Dear [firstname]

You may have received a letter from Ben, a student at the University of Bristol, congratulating you on your fantastic GCSE results. I'd like to add my congratulations! I am also studying at the University of Bristol – and wanted to follow up Ben's letter by reminding you that, with the grades you have achieved, you have more options open to you than most.

When I received my GCSE results in 2010, I had good grades and wanted to continue my education, but had no idea where to start looking. I decided to apply to university and after doing some research online and attending several open days I realised that there are so many opportunities to study at prestigious universities for students who have achieved grades like yours and mine.

I remember how difficult it was to choose a University. Each one is so different and you'll have many things to consider when deciding, such as the type of courses they offer and where they are based. The majority of people assume that the more prestigious universities are the most costly. This is not necessarily true, as these universities often provide larger grants or bursaries (money you are given and don't have to pay back) and government maintenance loans are more generous if you do choose to live away from home. I now live 200 miles from home, but have not suffered financially for doing so.

It's a very exciting time – but also important as the choices you make will affect your future. I would advise you to do plenty of research, visit open days and speak to students and lecturers. To remind you of the websites that can help, http://university.which.co.uk/ gives you honest advice about different places you could choose, www.gov.uk/student-finance and www.moneysavingexpert.com/students/student-loans-guide can help with any financial questions you may have.

I hope this letter helps you to realise that you've a great future ahead of you.

Yours sincerely,

_____

Research has shown that providing young people with better information on the costs and benefits of attending different universities helps them make better decisions about their future. The Department for Education has arranged for pupils that have performed very well in their GCSEs to receive letters from a current university student explaining how to find out more.

Both Ben and Rachel's letters were hand signed by their authors, and each letter was sent to more than 5,500 young people: Ben's in November, about a year before the students would need to apply to university, and Rachel's the following April.

Of the just over 11,000 young people in the country who met our criteria – both in terms of their grades and the school they were at – a quarter received Ben's letter, a quarter received Rachel's letter, and a quarter received both, with the remainder receiving neither letter, and just getting whatever support and encouragement they would have received from their schools anyway.

The effect of receiving both letters on applications to university was positive, but not significant. Applications to *selective* institutions, like Bristol (where Ben and Rachel studied) and other Russell Group universities, increased from 19.9 per cent to 23.2 per cent – a rise of 3.3 percentage points, or 16 per cent.

Similar interventions to make university easier for lower-income students have also found successes in the US. Caroline Hoxby and Sarah Turner from Stanford University found that providing personalized financial information to students, and making it easier to fill in application forms, significantly increased the number of universities to which they applied, and led to them applying to more selective institutions.[156] Most people who are nudged to apply, however, fall at the next hurdle – enrolment, or completing forms for financial aid – making it important to see whether people actually follow through.

Looking at the first test – whether or not universities make students offers – we find that they do; so it's not that the letters prompted applications from a group of people who didn't stand a chance of getting in. The effect follows through as far as our data goes – to offer acceptances, which are the best measure we have of whether someone actually attends a university. Given this, our best guess is that (compared to if no letters were sent) an extra 332 students attended a selective, Russell Group university – that's an increase of 35 per cent, and the entire intervention cost less than £1 ($1.5) per student.

The intervention also works best in the worst performing schools in the country,[157] and in the schools that have the least-well-off students[158] (these are fairly often the same schools)[159] – in some places doubling the rate of students being accepted to selective universities.

There are a number of competing theories as to what makes people respond to a role model. It could be that the role model helps to close the social distance we spoke about in Chapter 5, between the student and the idea of going to university. Alternatively, it could be a simple case of 'monkey see, monkey do'. Both of these theories are tempting, but are too simplistic to explain some of what we're seeing.

In Chapter 2 we saw the effects of stereotype threat on our ability to achieve our goals. To recap, stereotype threat strikes us when we're aware of a negative stereotype about a social group that we're a member of; for example, 'white boys from rural England struggle academically'. Our focus on the stereotype, even if we try to ignore it, draws energy and attention from what we're supposed to be doing, and can create a self-fulfilling prophecy.

Another, related, part of stereotype threat is from our own peers. We saw in Chapter 2 that young African Americans sometimes choose not to get as much education as they otherwise might to avoid being accused by their peers of 'acting white'. The fear of this accusation of in some way betraying your own group by aspiring to get an education can also contribute to the same threat response.

Prominently displaying role models, as we've shown above, can help to overcome stereotype threat through what Nilanjana Dasgupta, a social psychologist at the University of Massachusetts, calls a 'social vaccine'.[160] By providing an example of the stereotype being broken, the role models can help break the power of the stereotype.

If stereotype threat pervades our organizations in both the public and private sector, it means that groups with negative stereotypes are missing out and businesses and governments are foregoing valuable opportunities. It also means that it's not enough for companies to fix their own processes to weed out their own bias – we also need to help potential applicants to overcome the threat response.

Companies can help prospective employees by giving them real, relatable role models from their own group who can help close the social divide and show that the stereotype has already been broken. Groups that are under-represented in professional life, such as ethnic minorities, people from lower-income families, and women, could all be supported with access to role models.

This doesn't just apply in the run-up to employment, either. Once an employee is in the firm, they can still find the environment oppressive and difficult to manage if either social distance or stereotype threat are in their way. Mentoring and buddying with relatable role models could make a big difference to this, but so could drawing attention to leaders in the organization or even in the industry who are from their group.

When selecting a role model for your organization, there are a few things to consider. First, and unsurprisingly, shared social groups are important: male role models work better for men than female ones do, and vice versa; and a working-class white man is unlikely to reduce the social distance or fight stereotype threat for an African-American woman. This similarity might be difficult to manage, but the evidence seems to be that the tailoring will pay off in the end.

Second, proximity also seems to be important – this means picking role models who are relatable. As we've seen in Chapter 5, when thinking about reducing social distance, a role model who is *too* inspirational might not be effective. Picking someone who is achieving well but is just a few steps down the road from the person who we're seeking to inspire – a middle manager or successful member of the graduate training programme – is more likely to be effective than someone at the very top of the company, like the CEO. People who have risen from the very bottom to the very top are by definition exceptional. If you want to inspire someone to take up music, a local musician or member of a moderately famous band might be a better spur to action than Mozart or Taylor Swift, as it's easier to see yourself becoming fairly successful than it is to imagine being a once-in-a-generation success.*

Finally, not all role models are naturally good at role modelling, or want to do it, and this needs to be respected. In a study with HMRC, the British tax authority, we encouraged employees to donate to charity by showing them either a standard solicitation to donate, or a message from a role model, someone at HMRC who already made donations to charity.[161] Overall, the effects of the role model were positive, doubling the rate of signing up to

---

* This equivalence between Mozart and Taylor Swift may be controversial in some quarters, but we recommend that people give Mozart's work a second chance.

donate. However, not all role models are created equal. For people who received a message from one of the role models whose picture was clearly less appealing than the others, the message was actively off-putting, leading none of them to donate. In many cases, it will be worth sacrificing some of the personal touch in order to ensure that the role model is a good one.

In a study that we ran with the National Citizen Service – the volunteering programme for seventeen-year-olds that we mentioned in the last chapter – we compared three different ways of encouraging people to sign up to volunteer. The first was the business as usual: someone from NCS went into a school assembly and gave a short talk about the virtues of the programme. In the second condition, a young person who had been part of the programme the previous summer – an ambassador – came into the assembly to talk about their experience alongside the main speaker. And in the third group, a video of an ambassador was shown in assembly alongside the main speaker.

The third condition – the videoed role model – had been a last-minute addition to the design of the experiment, introduced because of the difficulty of arranging for ambassadors to be at schools at the right time. So we were quite surprised when the results came in and showed that the video had been more effective than the in-person speaker. In fact, the video increased sign-ups by 30 per cent, and the in-person ambassador actually decreased sign-ups slightly. More research is needed to be sure, but we think that this is because the in-person speaker had a few disadvantages: they had only one chance, they couldn't do repeated takes or practise very much, and they themselves had the stress associated with public speaking to contend with. The videoed ambassador would, we think, have been less compelling than a really good ambassador in person, but that quality is hard to judge in advance and really hard to ensure, so in the end the video looks like it comes out on top.

In this section we've looked at how to help people mobilize the social capital in their existing networks, to start to build new networks and, lastly, to start to imagine that they could move into new social environments and succeed there. We've seen that role models are a powerful influencer of what we see as being possible and appealing for us. Some people are lucky to be born with large numbers of role models in their networks already; but for others who don't, the good news is that we can bridge those gaps. Increasing the visibility of – and people's access to – people like them who are succeeding in the new environment (be it work, study, or the women's suffrage movement – remember Emmeline Pankhurst?) can inspire them to aspire to that themselves, and give them the confidence to make the decision and persist.

Organizations of all types could benefit from using role models to encourage and support aspiration in people who lack easy to access examples of successful people like them.

The benefits of stronger, broader social capital are tangible in terms of better educational outcomes, better employment outcomes and broadened horizons. However, they are also emotional and symbolic. In the next chapter, we look at two important elements of social capital: belonging and trusting, which is what happens when things go right.

13

Belonging and Trusting

'A map of the world that does not include Utopia is not
worth even glancing at, for it leaves out the one country at
which humanity is always landing.'

Oscar Wilde

W E WANT TO conclude by talking about two things that
happen when things go right, and why it's so important
that we continue to work towards a world that makes
the most of our social instincts: belongingness and social trust.
These two facets of our social selves are crucial to our wellbeing
as individuals, and to society's functioning.

Among all the stories of racist attacks, increased xenophobia
and populism in the political system that have been crowding
our airwaves (and were the focus of Part 1 of this book),
there's the story of a family of Sri Lankan Tamil refugees
who settled in the agricultural north of Queensland, Australia,
in a town called Biloela. Biloela has a population of fewer
than 6,000 people, is mainly white and English-speaking, and
since 2010 has been represented in the Federal Parliament by
the conservative Liberal National Party of Queensland. Priya,
Nades and their two daughters had lived in Biloela for four
years, and in March 2018, one day after Priya's visa expired, the

Australian Border Force raided their house and put the family in immigration detention, with the intention of deporting them to Sri Lanka.

The town of Biloela rallied behind the family, starting a petition that read: 'Please return this family to Biloela, their home, where they are wanted and welcome.'[162] About one hundred of the town's residents also flew to Melbourne (a journey of 1,200 miles) to the family's court hearing, and stood outside singing, 'I am, you are, we are Australian'.[163]

Belongingness refers to the formation of strong, stable and rewarding bonds between people.[164] but also to a broader sense of being accepted, valued and included by a group with which we identify,[165] like Priya and Nades are valued by the community of Biloela. In practice, it often comes down to a surprisingly simple question: 'Do you feel like you fit in here?' Many other things are packed into this, such as: 'Do you feel included in plans?', 'Do you feel accepted by and connected to others?' and 'Do you feel cared about?'

Think about a time when you've felt like you belonged. What did it feel like? For Michael, arriving at Harvard in 2014, it felt like being welcomed and valued. For Susannah, at the Australian Government Department of the Prime Minister and Cabinet in 2011, it felt like finding 'her people', who were interested in the same things she was, and who liked having the same kinds of conversations.

Psychologists classify the need to belong as one of our basic needs.[166] When something changes in our lives – either because we've moved into a new setting, or because something has changed in our current one – one of our main concerns will generally be about the bundle of questions that add up to 'belongingness'. And when it works out, the feeling of security and acceptance that comes with belonging can't be matched.

Perhaps that is why people have devoted pages and pages of books, and hours and hours of screen time, to protagonists' quests to find where they fit in, from the Pevensie siblings' discovery that they are the rightful kings and queens of Narnia, to Rory Gilmore's Yale journey in *Gilmore Girls*.

Maybe that is part of why the story of boy wizard Harry Potter – out-of-place, disliked by his family, friendless at school and with powers he didn't understand – captures our imagination. We can all identify with that feeling of being in the wrong place, or perhaps being the wrong person, of trying to make ourselves from a square peg into a round one to fit in with the people around us.

In the first novel in the bestselling series, Harry gets his Hogwarts letter and it turns out that the reason he's been so miserable is because *these aren't his people*. He gets swept into the literally magical world of wizarding Britain, where he is immediately welcomed, makes friends and acquires mentors. When he has to return to Little Whinging for the summer break, he never doubts that the wizarding world is where he belongs; and when the threat of Lord Voldemort arises, he fights without hesitation, because wizards are his people and they are facing an existential threat. Ultimately, Harry is willing to die for the sake of his group.

And belonging really matters. Studies have found associations between the sense of low belongingness and a range of mental and physical health issues, including depression, physical illness and substance use.[167] [168] Loneliness has even been associated with earlier death.[169] A sense of belonging is also associated with academic choices[170] and achievement[171] [172] and workplace performance,[173] including in high-stress work environments.[174]

Low belonging can also cause us to select out of groups that would otherwise be highly beneficial to us in terms of the social capital and networks they confer. Remember the case of a colleague from Chapter 2, who attended an interview where the panel and all the other interviewees were male, who ultimately declined the role because she felt like she wouldn't fit in?

But what makes people feel like they do – or don't – belong? The answer to that question draws on a lot of the things we've talked about in the book. We will feel like we belong in a group where we feel close to the 'ideal' member of that group, where the social cues we get are mostly that the group likes us and that we fit in, and where we feel like we're a core part of the network that makes up the group. Social support and social bridging help kick-start our belongingness by giving us a supportive environment and a fast-track to making friends. Role models help by giving some evidence that this is a place where people like us can fit in, which helps us to embark in the right mindset.

Likewise, belongingness is closely related to social capital: social capital brings with it belongingness and belongingness comes with social capital. Consider how attending a divisional meeting before moving to Canberra kickstarted Susannah's belongingness in her new job, which then led to her already knowing people when she moved to London; or how Harry Potter's parents' friends and well-wishers, like the Weasley family and Dumbledore, helped him settle in at Hogwarts. In this sense, belongingness is a goal end-state for a lot of the work we have talked about in the book.

Of course, some people feel the desire to belong more acutely than others. Every group has people who come and go and don't seem to feel a great deal of pressure to be included or to parrot the norms and shibboleths of the group (think Wolverine in the X-Men) and those who turn up reliably and toe the group line (Cyclops and Storm). But even Wolverine does seem to feel the benefits of belonging to the X-Men. And this might vary by group: we might feel a strong need to be recognized as a member of some groups and not others depending on how much we identify with them and how much we get out of group membership.

Research suggests that what really matters is not our level of need to belong, but whether or not our needs are being met.[175] So although Cyclops, Storm and Wolverine might all experience higher wellbeing from being in the X-Men, Cyclops or Storm would experience the loss of that belongingness more acutely than Wolverine because their need to belong was higher to start with, and would be keen to make sure that others were following the group's norms.

People with a high need to belong are also more sensitive to tonal cues and better at interpreting emotion,[176] but this can sometimes lead to over-interpretation. You may recall that in Chapters 1 and 2 we talked at length about different types of identity threat, one of which was a perceived threat to our affiliation to a valued group. Low-belongingness environments are those where an individual experiences a threat of rejection regularly, perhaps every day, from important figures in the environment, like their team leader, or the popular kids.[177] Over time, they argue, this forms into a hypothesis that 'people like me do not belong here'. And if we already have questions about whether we'll fit in, perhaps because we don't know anyone like us or because we don't really fit the stereotype of the group we're joining, then we may find it all too easy to find confirming evidence that we don't belong.

After the Brexit referendum on 23 June 2016, almost 4 million EU citizens living in the UK woke up feeling like they'd been 'living in someone else's house' and had outstayed their welcome.[178] According to the Office for National Statistics, 122,000 European citizens left the UK between March 2016 and March 2017 – including people who had been in the UK since they were children – reversing the trend of previous decades. The Here to Stay Project conducted a survey with 1,120 young Eastern Europeans in the UK. Lucie, a young Eastern European living in the UK, said, 'People who move here after Brexit will feel like they don't belong or are intruding, and no one should feel that way.'[179]

We agree with Lucie. Nobody should feel like they don't belong in settings they care about, where they have chosen and have a right to be. Most of this book so far has focused on how we can – through social choice architecture and strengthening their networks – influence individuals who in various contexts may feel like that. However, in this chapter we want to focus on the reverse – the arguably more important but also more challenging question of what individuals in a privileged position can do to help others know they're welcome, and that they belong.

The first challenge here is, of course, the increased polarization we explored in the first part of the book. There are many who actually don't want Europeans to feel like they belong in the UK, don't want Muslims to keep immigrating to Anglo-European countries or don't want to mix with those from working-class or non-white backgrounds at university. The reasons for this are worth exploring. On a practical level, increased inequality and flat economic growth create a situation in which people perceive that there are limited resources, and wherein the inclusion of others, whose need for resources might be greater, threatens their own access. This challenge is out of the hands of most social choice architects – it's a matter for the big levers of state: regulation, tax and welfare.

However, there are other reasons, which are more bound up with the work of this book and which may be more amenable to intervention.

As we have discussed in Chapter 4, lab research gives us some possible directions for investigation, particularly around strengthening people's identification with broader social groups like 'American' rather than 'Democrat' or 'Republican', identifying shared social groups like 'football fan', or encouraging situations where people can interact as individuals rather than members of social groups. In Chapter 4 we also saw some evidence that people who see their own identities as multifarious and complex show less stereotyping of people who are different to us and more tolerance. We wonder whether these types of identity interventions could encourage people to think about themselves and others in this way.

The power of role models and social bridging in this area are both interesting, in terms of their capacity to reduce the negative cues people receive for acting outside the norms of their groups. Finding role models to talk about embracing newcomers, from groups that have a strong identity, with heavily enforced norms, could be a powerful way to change what those social groups mean to members. For instance, we have talked about role models to encourage young people from working-class backgrounds to go to university, but what about role models of parents and friends who supported them to do so? Or role models of university students from traditional university-going backgrounds who embraced non-traditional students into their friendship groups?

Lastly, if we believe in the better world, we need to reach out to people who might be wondering whether they belong in it and make it clear that they do. We need to put aside our own social groups that make us different from each other and stand up for those who may be under attack. Like the people of Biloela, we need to say, loudly and often, 'You are wanted and welcome,' and we need to work to make that a reality.

Belonging is something that happens within us when things go right. The other side of the coin is social trust – something that happens between individuals, and between groups. We tend to think about trust in its most powerful, and perhaps more obvious form: the trust between the heroes in a buddy cop movie, or between family members. This kind of interpersonal trust is why Susannah is willing to leave her cat with our friend Kim when she goes away for a few nights, or why our friend Clare was willing to pay for *Hamilton* tickets for four people on her card, confident in the knowledge that we'd pay her back. This kind of trust is the sibling of belongingness: it's the product of strong, positive interpersonal relationships.

At the other extreme to this highly specific trust is what's known as social trust. Social trust is the amorphous sense that the world is safe – in fact, it's measured by a single question: 'Would you say that most people can be trusted? Or do you think you need to be very careful in dealing with others?' This question, with slight variations, has been asked by the World Values Survey (which, imaginatively, seeks to measure values, around the world, using a survey), the OECD, and by researchers trying to understand why some societies prosper and why some do not.

Trust is generally measured at a national level, but within countries there are microclimates of trust within towns or regions.

238

As the Harvard economist Andrei Schleifer[180] and his colleagues found, large organizations – big companies, or government departments, or hospitals – can also have their own, internal social trust, or a lack of it. Countries with low social trust seem to struggle to produce large, world-beating companies. That lack of trust at a national level makes it hard to work with people you don't know or see on a regular basis – so larger companies can't get going. For small firms, this means that increasing social trust – and hence the capacity to grow – could be a huge opportunity.

If Hogwarts does well to instil a sense of belonging among its students, and Harry in particular, it does a terrible job of building social trust. Most wizards' response to the question 'Do you believe that in general most people can be trusted?' would probably be 'Yes, unless they're a Slytherin, in which case absolutely not'. Of course, when a quarter of your school's defining characteristic is sneakiness, you're obviously going to experience issues with low trust. If the strong identities within the school's house system do not support this amorphous sense of trust, nor do many of its other institutions. The freedom with which heads of houses award points to their own houses is as striking as the rate at which they deduct them from others. Similarly, the repeated trend of Professor Dumbledore (a Gryffindor) conveniently awarding enough points to Gryffindor at the end of the school year so that they narrowly win, having been languishing behind, does not appear to encourage trust that the world is a fair and just place, and nor does the heavy gearing of the school's only sport (Quidditch) towards rewarding the acts of a single player with both victory and glory. Although the drama at Hogwarts implicitly revolves around the Slytherin v Gryffindor rivalry, both groups are beneficiaries of an unequal system, with neither of the other houses having won the house cup in our lifetimes.[181]

Bo Rothstein, a Swedish political scientist whose research outlines the importance of institutions, like a government, or the house cup, for encouraging trust, points out that trends towards lower trust are hard to reverse once they've become embedded. He points to two economic factors that help shape social trust: economic equality, which we can think about in terms of how big the gap is between rich and poor, and equality of opportunity, which is the extent to which your parents' wealth determines how well you do in life.

The more equal your society is, Rothstein argues, the more likely that society is to be one with high trust – in part because these societies are likely to lower levels of social distance between different people, and threats to individuals' identities from rival groups may be more limited. More equal societies, even if people are equally poor, experience a lower sense that things aren't fair and that the dice are loaded in favour of some people (Gryffindor, Slytherin) and against some others (Hufflepuff and Ravenclaw).

Let's say that a government wants to increase social trust. As with belongingness, the prescription seems pretty clear – just increase equality. Easily done, right? As Rothstein and Eric Uslaner argue, not so much. If we're going to increase equality, some redistribution, either of wealth or of opportunity, is going to be necessary.

Universal, or near-universal benefits, like the Earned Income Tax Credit in the US or Child Benefit in the UK, have the advantage of having a broad base of support, making them hard for any government to unpick without suffering a backlash from across society. They're also a smoother way to redistribute wealth from the top of the system to the bottom than more targeted interventions, as they don't experience big drops in the same way as, for example, unemployment benefits.[182] They appear to be 'fair', too, because to a certain extent everyone benefits from them (as opposed to, for instance, Dumbledore redistributing points to Gryffindor).

Redistributing opportunity is harder than moving money or points around, but follows the same principles. A universal benefit – like free comprehensive education – helps to give everyone access to the same opportunities, at least in education. If you also banned some of the major sources of educational inequality like fee-paying private schools or selective grammar schools then you'd expect to see a society in which opportunity was more evenly spread.

In a low-trust society, however, these policies are pretty hard to achieve. If there's low trust, the poor might think that the rich's wealth is ill-gotten, and resist a universal benefit, as it doesn't sufficiently penalize the wealthy. Elsewhere, people in a low-trust society are more likely to make a distinction between the deserving and undeserving poor – between 'strivers' and 'scroungers', for example – and wish to target benefits at the former, while sanctioning the latter for their lack of moral fibre.

Increasing trust is therefore a big challenge for governments. Not only does it typically require aggressive use of taxation or legislation, but also countries can get into a trust trap, in which trust is so low that they can't take the necessary steps to increase it. Changing the microclimates within organizations might actually be easier to achieve.

There are some concrete actions that we can take within organizations to help escape the trust trap using behavioural science. Our perception of inequality between groups is in part a consequence of the hard dividing lines between groups and the decline in shared social groups. Just as the formation of the (exclusively Slytherin) Inquisitorial Squad led to the further disintegration of trust between the Hogwarts houses, the growing sense of 'us' and 'them' makes us less trusting.

As we mentioned at the start of this book, our research suggests that, as with belongingness, a part of the way to boost trust might be to break down these barriers between members of different groups – in the case of that study, by getting people to reflect on their similarities rather than their differences. An alternative might be found in the creation of 'rituals' that create a common sense of shared identity within an organization and increase our sense that we overlap with others. In BIT's New York office, for example, when a new study launches, they ring a bell. It lets everyone share in the successes of the team; and the first time you ring the bell, you know you're part of the team.

We could similarly make use of social cues about the importance of fairness. Just as someone with a broom creates a salient cue that cleanliness is important, elevating trustworthy individuals and punishing those who deviate from norms of fairness, particularly in senior positions, could make a big difference. Even if that means firing Dumbledore for blatant favouritism.

Although practical, these interventions alone are probably not going to move the needle on social trust if the barriers between groups still exist – and social bridging shows the most potential here. Programmes like the National Citizen Service in the UK – the large-scale volunteering programme for seventeen-year-olds in the UK that we saw back in Chapter 11 – which deliberately bring together people from a wide variety of backgrounds and expose them to situations very different from their own, seem to be effective at breaking down these barriers, with behavioural science interventions like buddying helping to boost their effectiveness. It will take a long time for even something as large as the NCS to infect all of society, however, and today's seventeen-year-olds to rise to positions of power before we realize the benefits that these programmes promise. Instead, infusing social bridging through all of our institutions, from governments to universities to companies, is behavioural science's best current chance to build social trust and move towards a more utopian world.

Conclusion

T HIS IS A very different book to the one that we set out to write almost a year ago. From our experiences working at the Behavioural Insights Team, and latterly at King's College London, we had a fairly positive view of the power of social influence to make the world a better place. All of our research, and that which we read, was full of people engaging in acts of kindness to one another.

Over the course of the year, a few things happened to alter that view. First, the world itself has changed. During the time in which we've been writing this book, the extent of Cambridge Analytica and the Russian government's collusion, tacit or otherwise, with both the Brexit and Trump campaigns has become much more obvious, and the level of interest in the press, in government and among academics, in fake news has understandably skyrocketed. Even as we set out to write a book about how well-intentioned institutions could boost social connectedness and lead to better outcomes in health, education and work, those very same institutions were seemingly falling apart, or at the very least proving themselves underprepared and ill-equipped to defend our democracies from this tide of abuse.

Second, we came to realize that we were living in an echo-chamber, where we could see all the good that was going on and instinctively viewed the rise of our understanding of social influence as a good thing, with the benefits outweighing the costs. Living day in, day out, conducting the kind of research that we do, makes it easy for us to see this as just the way things are. Talking to friends and family, however, we understood that the common perspective was very different. Social influence, to them, meant conformity, and the notion of governments using psychological pressure to encourage particular sorts of behaviour felt to them quite a lot like propaganda. Over the year, the more generic questions we'd previously been asked about our work ('Is that ethical?') gave way to more specific ones: 'How are you like Cambridge Analytica?' and 'Did you have anything to do with Brexit?'

Finally, we were aware that the prevailing wind of the literature on social capital was against us, painting an often dispiriting picture of low social mobility, and of declining social capital. Against this backdrop, and the sense that things were getting worse, and not better, how are nudges and other behavioural interventions going to have any kind of impact?

We couldn't ignore what we were seeing in the world around us, and so we started this book with a vision that many would call dystopian. Indeed, many commentators have mused over the past two years that we must be living in the 'darkest timeline', a reference to multiverse theory,* which posits that there are infinite parallel universes that capture all possible configurations of every possible decision every human has made. If that's true, then at least we can hope there's a parallel universe out there where the social and political landscape looks very different to how it does in 'our' 2019 – and perhaps even one where people have discovered the secret of being kind on the internet.

---

* Via the TV show *Community*.

In Part 1, we explored the ways in which we form social groups and use them to divide and separate ourselves from others, to exclude those who are not like us. The fracturing of society, the 'post-Truth' world, declining social trust, declining connections between people, and all of it in the pressure cooker of the online world. Most chillingly, we saw how our social instincts can be manipulated and used to steer us in undesirable directions against our will and without our knowledge.

But we're optimists, and hope that in this book we've started to plot out a map that, if it doesn't get us all the way to Utopia at least gets us into its general vicinity. From Part 2 of this book onwards, we've hopefully seen that we're probably not, in fact, in 'the darkest timeline' – although it would perhaps be all too easy to get there. Instead, Parts 2 and 3 have shown a pathway to a brighter set of scenarios, in which our social selves seek out others to belong with, while generally trusting those around us to do the right thing. By learning from the norms and cues in our environment, and from the people in our networks, by dwelling on the parts of ourselves that are similar to others, and not the ways in which we are different, we can find ourselves in one of those brighter worlds. And as architects of those environments and networks – as managers, policymakers, family and friends – we can help to harness those powers for good.

Despite this, our infrastructure to make this happen is lacking. The networks we have in society at the moment may not inevitably lead us to the darkest world, but they limit how much light can be let in. Radical change can be expensive to attain, but spending money is, as we've seen time and time again, no guarantee of success. There is a growing body of evidence suggesting that a few lighter interventions, such as social support, role models and social bridging, can help make up for deficiencies in our existing networks, and even help us to build new and more effective ones.

It's taken forty years for the behavioural revolution to supplant the rational model in economics, and for economists to accept that, in the words of Ken Binmore, 'in the long run we're all stupid'. Accepting a social revolution, and that our networks and identities are as important as our preferences and beliefs, should take much less time. After all, as we've seen, following the social is something we do naturally.

Our favourite thing about these insights is that, unlike the Moving to Opportunity programme, or the National Citizen Service, they can be applied cheaply and scaled up quickly. As we've seen throughout the book, organizations like schools, governments, universities and companies are home to their own forms of social capital, and their own opportunities to tweak the social choice architecture.

There are a few things that we think are shovel-ready and pretty easy to deploy.

First, you should consider what people are going to pick up from their environment. We've seen that people are very responsive both to what other people are doing (see Chapter 6), and what the environment itself tells them (Chapter 7). If the office is untidy, or if people are seen to disrespect it, people automatically internalize this. If there's a culture of office gossip, or of secrecy, then even the most taciturn of us might indulge just to blend in.

Second, we should think about who goes into teams and their first interactions. As we saw in Chapter 5, more diverse groups are better but people are less comfortable in them – so exercises like the ice-breakers we've shown, such as getting people to talk about the things that make them similar, or an appeal to a 'higher' group (like Londoners, or Mets fans) can help make the group easier to handle. If you've got people joining an established group from outside, you might want to think about going one step further and use something like a buddy scheme to help them build a link into the team before they join.

Third, a successful leader or manager is probably one who is, in addition to focusing on building staff skills in the workplace, helping them to build and manage their social capital. This goes beyond simply encouraging office activities like yoga, or networking drinks after work. Letting information about these activities move through the office network organically, having been seeded with a few well-connected people, might also make them more effective than a simple top-down pronouncement. When people struggle to take part, either because they're nervous or because they're not sure they're the intended audience, we can encourage and promote others who might take a prominent place as a role model or just as a friend. Even if you don't see it as your place to help build people's social capital, just getting them to think about who in their existing networks can support them could make a difference.

Finally – and this might be the hardest one – don't be afraid to start again. As we saw in Chapter 8, toxic environments can persist long after the people who began them have left, because the group itself remembers. If a team or social group has a very negative relationship with another, like we saw in Chapter 1, or very clearly polices who is 'in' and who is 'out' of the social group, it may be time to split that team up and start again. If you're in a management or leadership position, you might be amazed by how much influence you can have via these social channels.

It's very easy to think that there's nothing to be done to change things: humans are wired to see 'us' and 'them'; that discrimination is printed in our DNA and there's nothing that can be done about it. But stories like that of Priya and Nades in the last chapter remind us that, as the film director Richard Curtis says, we should be suspicious of the romanticization of bad things. The bad things that happen may be more obvious, and may draw more attention and column inches, but the positives are more plentiful – and, lest we forget, our social instincts are the building blocks of all modern (and ancient) civilization. Although there are indeed terrible things happening in the modern world that will vex us all for years to come, the overwhelming majority of acts, by the overwhelming majority of people, are positive. We mustn't lose sight of that, nor stop working towards a better, fairer, more social world.

NOTES

Introduction

1. Kahneman, D. and Tversky, A. (1979). 'Prospect theory: An analysis of decision under risk', *Econometrica, 47(2)*, 263.
2. For pedants, yes: this is technically the Swedish National Bank's Prize in Economic Sciences in Memory of Alfred Nobel, rather than a 'true' Nobel Prize.
3. Thaler, R. H. and Sunstein, C. R. (2008). *Nudge: Improving decisions about health, wealth and happiness.* New Haven, CT: Yale University Press.

PART 1: THE STATE OF SOCIAL INFLUENCE

1: Them

4. Tajfel, H. (1981). The development of a perspective. In *Human groups and social categories: Studies in social psychology* (pp. 1–3). Cambridge, UK: Cambridge University Press.
5. Turner, J. C. (1996). Henri Tajfel: An introduction. In W. P. Robinson (Ed.), *Social groups and identities: Developing the legacy of Henri Tajfel.* Oxford, UK: Butterworth-Heinemann.
6. Bertrand, M. and Mullainathan, S. (2004). Are Emily and Greg more employable than Lakisha and Jamal? A field experiment on labor market discrimination. *American Economic Review, 94(4)*, 991–1013.
7. Taifel, H. (1970). Experiments in intergroup discrimination. *Scientific American*, 223(5), 96–103.
8. Sherif, M., Harvey, O. J., White, B. J., Hood, W. R., Sherif, C. W. (1961). *Intergroup conflict and cooperation: The Robbers Cave*

experiment (pp.150–98). Norman, OK: University Book Exchange.

9. Iyengar, S., Sood, G., & Lelkes, Y. (2012). Affect, not ideology: A social identity perspective on polarization. *Public Opinion Quarterly, 76*(3), 405–431.

10. Major, B., Blodorn, A. & Blascovich, G. M. (2016). The threat of increasing diversity: Why many White Americans support Trump in the 2016 presidential election. *Group Processes & Intergroup Relations.* doi: 10.1177/1368430216677304.

11. Mason, L. & Wronski, J. (2018). One tribe to bind them all: How our social group attachments strengthen partisanship. *Political Psychology, 39*(S1), 257–77.

12. Cohn, N. (2017, March 28). A 2016 review: Turnout wasn't the driver of Clinton's defeat. *New York Times,* p. A17. Retrieved from https://www.nytimes.com/2017/03/28/upshot/a-2016-review-turnout-wasnt-the-driver-of-clintons-defeat.html

13. This is known in the literature as 'derogation'.

14. Maass, A., Cadinu, M., Guarnieri, G., & Grasselli, A. (2003). Sexual harassment under social identity threat: The computer harassment paradigm. *Journal of personality and social psychology, 85*(5), 853.

15. Newheiser, A. K., Barreto, M., & Tiemersma, J. (2017). People like me don't belong here: Identity concealment is associated with negative workplace experiences. *Journal of Social Issues, 73*(2), 341–58.

2: Us

16. Quotation from Dreyfus, A. (1901). *Five Years of My Life, 1894–1899.* New York, NY: McClure, Phillips & Co. Image from cover of French newspaper *Le Petit Journal* (1895, January 13). Le Traitre: Degradation d'Alfred Dreyfus. *Le Petit Journal,* p. 1.

17. Ouwerkerk, J. W., Kerr, N. L., Gallucci, M., & Van Lange, P. A. (2005). Avoiding the social death penalty: Ostracism and cooperation in social dilemmas. In K. D. Williams, J. P. Forgas & W. von Hippel (Eds.), *The social outcast: Ostracism, social exclusion, rejection, and bullying* (pp.321–32). New York, NY; Psychology Press.

18. Hartgerink, C. H. J., van Beest, I., Wicherts, J. M., & Williams, K. D. (2015). The ordinal effects of ostracism: A meta-analysis of

120 cyberball studies. *PLoS ONE, 10*(5), 1–24. DOI: doi:10.1371/journal. pone.0127002.

19. Zadro, L., & Richardson, R. (2004). How low can you go? Ostracism by a computer is sufficient to lower self-reported levels of belonging, control, self-esteem, and meaningful existence. *Journal of Experimental Social Psychology, 40*(10), 560–7.

20. Levett-Jones, T., & Lathlean, J. (2009).'Don't rock the boat': Nursing students' experiences of conformity and compliance. *Nurse Education Today, 29*(1), 342–9.

21. Fryer, R. G. F., & Torelli, P. (2010). An empirical analysis of 'acting white'. *Journal of Public Economics, 94*(1), 380–96.

22. Austen-Smith, D. & Fryer, R. G. (2004). An economic analysis of 'acting white' (No. 1399). Evanston, IL: Centre for Mathematical Studies in Economics and Management Science.

23. In fact, almost all ethnic minorities outperform white British students on most attainment measures.

24. Ward, M. K., & Broniarczyk, S. M. (2011). It's not me, it's you: How gift giving creates giver identity threat as a function of social closeness. *Journal of Consumer Research*, *38*(1), 164–81.

25. Gino, F., Ayal, S., & Ariely, D. (2009). Contagion and differentiation in unethical behavior: The effect of one bad apple on the barrel. *Psychological Science*, *20*(3), 393–8.

3: Manipulation

26. Deloitte (2017). *State of the Smart: Global Mobile Consumer Survey 2017: UK Cut* (p.12). London, United Kingdom: Deloitte LLP. Retrieved from http://www.deloitte.co.uk/mobileuk/assets/img/download/global-mobile-consumer-survey-2017_uk-cut.pdf

27. Deloitte (2017). *State of the Smart: Global Mobile Consumer Survey 2017: UK Cut* (p.12). London, United Kingdom: Deloitte LLP. Retrieved from http://www.deloitte.co.uk/mobileuk/assets/img/download/global-mobile-consumer-survey-2017_uk-cut.pdf

28. Pew Research Center. (2017). *Mobile fact sheet*. Washington, DC: Pew Research Center. Retrieved from http://www.pewinternet.org/fact-sheet/mobile/

29. Whillans, A. V., Christie, C. D., Cheung, S., Jordan, A. H., and Chen,

F. S. (2017). From misperception to social connection: Correlates and consequences of overestimating others' social connectedness. *Personality and Social Psychology Bulletin, 43*(12), 1696–711.

30. Answer: not really.

31. Answer: a bit.

32. Bond, R. M., Fariss, C. J., Jones, J. J., Kramer, A. D. I., Marlow, C., Settle, J. E., & Fowler, J. H. (2012). A 61-million-person experiment in social influence and political mobilization. *Nature, 489*, 291–8.

33. There are a few possible explanations for this, including that people don't really have a sense of whether telling Facebook you voted means anything (people can lie), and what constitutes a large number of people doing this.

34. Pictures taken from the article by Bond et al. (2012).

35. The researchers class a 'close friend' based on the amount of Facebook interaction two people have being in the top 10 per cent for all users. About 99 per cent of users have at least one close friend under this definition.

36. Meko, T., Lu, D., and Gamio, L. (2016, November 11). How Trump won the presidency with razor-thin margins in swing states. *The Washington Post*. Retrieved from https://www.washingtonpost.com/graphics/politics/2016-election/swing-state-margins

37. Taken from Friggeri et al. (2014).

38. Although they did find that humorous memes, and those that mock the original, false, premise, spread faster and are more effective than more serious corrections.

39. Pennycook, G., & Rand, D. G. (2018). Lazy, not biased: Susceptibility to partisan fake news is better explained by lack of reasoning than by motivated reasoning. *Cognition*.

40. Cadwalladr, C. & Graham-Harrison, E. (2018, March 17). Revealed: 50 million Facebook profiles harvested for Cambridge Analytica in major data breach. *The Guardian*. Retrieved from https://www.theguardian.com/news/2018/mar/17/cambridge-analytica-facebook-influence-us-election

41. 'Senator, we run ads.'

42. Unlike Canute, they may believe that they are able to do so through incisive questioning, however.

PART 2: NUDGES

4: Social Groups

43. Turner, J. C. (1999). Some current issues in research on social identity and self-categorization theories. *Social Identity: Context, Commitment, Content,* 3(1), 6–34. See also Haslam, S. A., & Platow, M.J. (2001). Your wish is our command: The role of shared social identity in translating a leader's vision into followers' action. In M.A. Hogg & D.J. Terry (Eds), *Social Identity Processes in Organizational Contexts* (pp. 213-228). Philadelphia, PA: Psychology Press.
44. Hogg, M. A., & Reid, S. A. (2006). Social identity, self-categorization, and the communication of group norms. *Communication Theory,* 16(1), 17–30.
45. This is a broad simplification.
46. Meaning she worked providing policy advice within a government department.
47. https://cpb-us-w2.wpmucdn.com/voices.uchicago.edu/dist/b/232/files/2016/09/PNAS-2016-Bryan-10830-5-1t6bc4p.pdf
48. http://citeseerx.ist.psu.edu/viewdoc/download?doi=10.1.1.847.2320&rep=rep1&type=pdf
49. https://bingschool.stanford.edu/sites/default/files/publications/bryanetal2014_0.pdf
50. Brewer, M. B., & Pierce, K. P. (2005). Social Identity Complexity and Outgroup Tolerance. *Personality and Social Psychology Bulletin,* 31(3), 428–37.
51. Comer, J. (1988). *Maggie's American Dream: The Life and Times of a Black Family.* New York: New American Library.
52. Brewer, M. B., & Pierce, K. P. (2005). Social identity complexity and outgroup tolerance. *Personality and Social Psychology Bulletin,* 31(3), 428–37.
53. Aron, A., Melinat, E., Aron, E. N., Vallone, R. D., & Bator, R. J. (1997). The experimental generation of interpersonal closeness: A procedure and some preliminary findings. *Personality and Social Psychology Bulletin,* 23(4), 363–77.
54. https://www.annualreviews.org/doi/pdf/10.1146/annurev.psych.60.110707.163607

55. https://www.ssoar.info/ssoar/bitstream/handle/document/22771/ssoar-gpir-2005-2-galinsky_et_al-perspective-taking_and_self-other_overlap_fostering.pdf?sequence=1

5: Social Distance

56. Kahneman, D., Knetsch, J. L., & Thaler, R. H. (1986). 'Fairness and the assumptions of economics', *Journal of Business, 59*(4), S285–S300.
57. This paper was published in 1986. So 210 years after the publication of the Wealth of Nations, and the foundation of modern economics, economists worked out that people care about each other – and even after that long we still needed help from psychologists like Daniel Kahneman.
58. Charness, G., and Gneezy, U. (2003). 'What's in a name? Anonymity and social distance in dictator and ultimatum games', *Journal of Economic Behaviour and Organisation, 68*(1), 29–35.
59. This isn't technically true. Unlike psychologists, who can deceive participants or use confederates to steer the outcome in a particular direction, economists running lab experiments are banned from being anything other than truthful with their participants about any part of the experiment. If an experiment is found to have deceived people, not only will it be unpublishable but also the entire lab risks being blacklisted for evermore.
60. Calculated using data from Carnevale, A. P., Rose, S. J., and Cheah, B. (2011). *The college payoff: Education, occupations, lifetime earnings.* Washington, DC: The Georgetown University Centre on Education and the Workforce.
61. Coughlan, S. (2017, July 5). 'Student debt rising to more than £50,000, says IFS', *BBC News.* Retrieved from http://www.bbc.co.uk/news/education-40493658
62. UK Government (2018). 'Percentile points from 1 to 99 for total income before and after tax'. Retrieved from https://www.gov.uk/government/statistics/percentile-points-from-1-to-99-for-total-income-before-and-after-tax
63. Warrell, H. (2017, July 5). 'Three-quarters of graduates "will never repay student loans"', *Financial Times.* Retrieved from https://www.ft.com/content/3fc14332-60c7-11e7-8814-0ac7eb84e5f1

64. Harvard College (2018). 'Harvard at a glance'. Retrieved from https://www.harvard.edu/about-harvard/harvard-glance

65. University of Oxford (2017). 'Oxford thinking: The campaign for the University of Oxford'. Retrieved from https://www.campaign. ox.ac.uk/the-campaign

66. Small, D. A., and Loewenstein, G. (2003). 'Helping *a* victim or helping *the* victim: Altruism and identifiability', *The Journal of Risk and Uncertainty, 26*(1), 5–16.

67. Paraphrasing Jeremy Bentham.

68. Kogut, T., and Ritov, I. (2005). 'The "identified victim" effect: An identified group, or just a single individual?', *Journal of Behavioural Decision Making, 18*(3), 157–67.

69. Page 146. Small, D. A., Loewenstein, G., and Slovic, P. (2007). 'Sympathy and callousness: The impact of deliberative thought on donations to identifiable and statistical victims', *Organizational Behaviour and Human Decision Processes, 102*(2), 143–153.

70. Harvard Business Review Staff. (2014, November). 'Cooks make tastier food when they can see their customers', *Harvard Business Review*. Retrieved from (https://hbr.org/2014/11/ cooks-make-tastier-food-when-they-can-see-their-customers

71. Correct as of 4 November 2017.

72. Galinsky, A., Todd, A., Homan, K., Apfelbaum, E., Sasaki, S. Richeson, J. Olayon, J. and Maddux, W. 2015. Maximizing the gains and minimizing the pains of diversity: A policy perspective. *Perspectives in Psychological Science,*

73. HarvardCPL, YouTube (2016). 'BX2016 "Making Diversity Work" Plenery'. Retrieved from https://www.youtube.com/watch?v=Fz69k7Y-hP0&list=PLFBI1oxoPcgk-OemGNhGnewSmaPBOlswZ

74. Phillips, K. W. (2014, October 1). 'How diversity makes us smarter', *Scientific American*. Retrieved from https://www.scientificamerican. com/article/how-diversity-makes-us-smarter/

75. Although not as cheap as economists think. Richard Thaler and colleagues found when analysing behaviour on the TV show *Golden Balls* that people who promised not to betray their competitors were much less likely to actually do so than people who didn't explicitly promise.

76. For those unfamiliar with the idea, there are a few variants on the Secret Santa theme but the main premise allows large groups of people

to celebrate Christmas by exchanging gifts without the potentially crippling financial burden (not to mention angst) of buying individual presents for everyone. Each person buys *one* present, either for a specific individual or for the pool, and these gifts are then distributed by a central force, with the point being that nobody knows who was assigned to whom, or who bought which gift.

6: Social Norms

77. Fandom (2018). Memory alpha: 'In the cards' (episode). Retrieved from http://memory-alpha.wikia.com/wiki/In_the_Cards_(episode)

78. Falk, A., Fischbacher, U., & Gächter, S. (2010). Living in two neighbourhoods: Social interaction effects in the laboratory. *Economic Inquiry, 51*(1), 563–78.

79. A particular favourite is called 'Black Rat', which is rumoured to actually be made with said animal.

80. https://www.telegraph.co.uk/news/2018/01/29/black-cats-shunned-rescue-shelter-dont-look-good-selfies/

81. Banerjee, A. V. (1992). A simple model of herd behaviour. *The Quarterly Journal of Economics, 107*(3), 797–817.

82. Glinski, R. J., Glinski, B. C., & Slatin, G. T. (1970). Nonnaivety contamination in conformity experiments: Sources, effects, and implications for control. *Journal of Personality and Social Psychology, 16*(3), 478–85.

83. Schroeder, C. M., & Prentice, D. A. (1998). Exposing Pluralistic Ignorance to Reduce Alcohol Use Among College Students 1. *Journal of Applied Social Psychology, 28*(23), 2150–80.

84. Canning, A., Hume, S., Makinson, L., Koponen, M., Hall, K., & Delargy, C. (2018). *KCLxBIT Project Report 2015-2017: Behavioural insights in higher education @KCLxBIT.* London, UK: the Behavioural Insights Team and King's College London.

85. Hallsworth, M., List, J. A., Metcalfe, R. D., & Vlaev, I. (2017). The behaviouralist as tax collector: Using natural field experiments to enhance tax compliance. *Journal of Public Economics, 148*, 14–31.

86. Kettle, S., Hernandez, M., Ruda, S., & Sanders, M. (2016). *Behavioural interventions in tax compliance: Evidence from Guatemala.* (World Bank Policy Research working paper no. 7690). Washington, DC: World Bank.

87. Goldstein, N. J., Cialdini, R. B., & Griskevicius, V. (2008). A room with a viewpoint: Using social norms to motivate environmental conservation in hotels. *Journal of Consumer Research*, *35*(3), 472–82.

88. Allcott, H. (2011). Social norms and energy conservation. *Journal of Public Economics*, *95*(9), 1082–95.

89. Alpizar, Francisco, Fredrik Carlsson, and Olof Johansson-Stenman. 'Anonymity, reciprocity, and conformity: Evidence from voluntary contributions to a national park in Costa Rica.' *Journal of Public Economics* 92, no. 5–6 (2008): 1047–1060.

90. Just Giving (2017). Carlos' sponsored beard shaving! Retrieved from https://www.justgiving.com/campaigns/charity/qahh/beard-be-gone

91. Just Giving (2018). Beans on Jake. Retrieved from https://www.justgiving.com/fundraising/beansonjake

92. This phenomenon, of following one virtuous act with another, 'sinful' act – like having pudding after going for a run – is called *moral licensing*, and is one reason that many physical-activity programmes fail. Moral licensing is particularly dangerous in combination with other self-serving biases: research by Daniel Effron from London Business School shows that while we try to substitute our virtue for our vice, we're incredibly good at lying to ourselves about how much exercise we *really* did, and pretty clueless about how many calories we *actually* burned.

93. Jakicic, J. M., Davis, K. K., Rogers, R. J., King, W. C., Marcus, M. D., Helsel, D., .& Belle, S. H. (2016). Effect of wearable technology combined with a lifestyle intervention on long-term weight loss: the IDEA randomized clinical trial. *Jama*, *316*(11), 1161–71.

94. Hallsworth, M., Chadborn, T., Sallis, A., Sanders, M., Berry, D., Greaves, F., Clements, L., & Davies, S. C. (2016). Provision of social norm feedback to high prescribers of antibiotics in general practice: A pragmatic national randomised controlled trial. *The Lancet*, *387*(10029), 1743–52.

7: Social Cues

95. Some theorists use the distinction of 'descriptive social norms', which we covered in the last chapter, and 'injunctive social norms', which are more about our overall sense of what actions would be approved of or disapproved of by our group. This chapter covers

some cues that build up our sense of what the injunctive social norms are, but also ranges a bit more broadly.

96. In 2018 the UK government issued advice to pause such redesigns, since the removal of kerbs and crossing-points can be hazardous for visually impaired people.

97. Large infrastructure projects are also difficult to robustly evaluate, and the large amounts of financial and political capital involved mean people are usually pretty keen to say they've been a huge success – not a good candidate for the behavioural insights approach!

98. Millward, L. J., Haslam, S. A., & Postmes, T. (2007). Putting employees in their place: The impact of hot desking on organizational and team identification. *Organization Science, 18*(4), 547–59.

99. Hirst, A. (2011). Settlers, vagrants and mutual indifference: unintended consequences of hot-desking. *Journal of Organizational Change Management, 24*(6), 767–88.

100. Authors own calculations based on Table 2 of John et al (2010). Participants are 98 per cent more likely to admit to immoral or suspect behaviours on an unprofessional website.

101. John, L. K., Acquisti, A., & Loewenstein, G. (2010). Strangers on a plane: Context-dependent willingness to divulge sensitive information. *Journal of consumer research, 37*(5), 858–73.

102. Of course, their disclosures *were* treated anonymously and safely in all conditions!

103. Aarts, H., & Dijksterhuis, A. (2003). The silence of the library: Environment, situational norm, and social behaviour. *Journal of Personality and Social Psychology, 84*(1), 18.

104. Henrich, J., McElreath, R., Barr, A., Ensminger, J., Barrett, C., Bolyanatz, A., & Lesorogol, C. (2006). Costly punishment across human societies. *Science, 312*(5781), 1767–70.

105. Ostrom, E., Burger, J., Field, C. B., Norgaard, R. B., & Policansky, D. (1999). Revisiting the commons: local lessons, global challenges. *Science, 284*(5412), 278–82.

106. Ostrom, E. (2000). Collective action and the evolution of social norms. *Journal of Economic Perspectives, 14*(3), 137–158.

107. Berndt, T. J. (1979). Developmental changes in conformity to peers and parents. *Developmental Psychology, 15*(6), 608.

108. Yeager, D. S., Purdie-Vaughns, V., Garcia, J., Apfel, N., Brzustoski,

P., Master, A., Hessert, W. T., Williams, M. E., & Cohen, G. L. (2014). Breaking the cycle of mistrust: Wise interventions to provide critical feedback across the racial divide. *Journal of Experimental Psychology: General, 143*(2), 804.

109. Ruck, M. D., & Wortley, S. (2002). Racial and ethnic minority high school students' perceptions of school disciplinary practices: A look at some Canadian findings. *Journal of Youth and Adolescence, 31*(3), 185–95.

110. Urhahne, D. (2015). Teacher behaviour as a mediator of the relationship between teacher judgment and students' motivation and emotion. Teaching and Teacher Education, 45, 73–82.

111. Van den Bergh, L., Denessen, E., Hornstra, L., Voeten, M., & Holland, R. W. (2010). The implicit prejudiced attitudes of teachers: Relations to teacher expectations and the ethnic achievement gap. *American Educational Research Journal, 47*(2), 497–527.

112. Biernat, M., & Manis, M. (1994). Shifting standards and stereotype-based judgments. *Journal of Personality and Social Psychology, 66*(1), 5.

113. Carroll Massey, G., Vaughn Scott, M., & Dornbusch, S. M. (1975). Racism without racists: Institutional racism in urban schools. *The Black Scholar, 7*(3), 10–19.

114. Cohen, G. L., Steele, C. M., & Ross, L. D. (1999). The mentor's dilemma: Providing critical feedback across the racial divide. *Personality and Social Psychology Bulletin, 25*(10), 1302–18.

115. Yeager, D. S., Purdie-Vaughns, V., Garcia, J., Apfel, N., Brzustoski, P., Master, A., Hessert, W. T., Williams, M. E., & Cohen, G. L. (2014). Breaking the cycle of mistrust: Wise interventions to provide critical feedback across the racial divide. *Journal of Experimental Psychology: General, 143*(2), 804.

116. Frey, B. S., & Oberholzer-Gee, F. (1997). The cost of price incentives: An empirical analysis of motivation crowding-out. *The American Economic Review, 87*(4), 746–55.

117. Le Grand, J. (2003). Motivation, agency, and public policy: Of knights and knaves, pawns and queens. Oxford, UK: Oxford University Press on Demand.

118. Braga, A. A., Welsh, B. C., & Schnell, C. (2015). Can policing disorder reduce crime? A systematic review and meta-analysis. *Journal of Research in Crime and Delinquency, 52*(4), 567–88.

119. Wikipedia (2018). Stop-and-frisk in New York City. Retrieved from https://en.wikipedia.org/wiki/Stop-and-frisk_in_New_York_City#Studies_on_the_effects

120. Petrosino, A., Turpin-Petrosino, C., Hollis-Peel, M. E., & Lavenberg, J. G. (2013). 'Scared Straight' and other juvenile awareness programs for preventing juvenile delinquency. *Cochrane Database of Systematic Reviews.* doi 10.1002/14651858. CD002796.pub2\

121. Petrosino, A., Guckenburg, S., & Turpin-Petrosino, C. (2010). Formal system processing of juveniles: Effects of delinquency. Washington, DC: US Department of Justice. https://campbellcollaboration.org/library/formal-system-processing-of-juveniles-effects-on-delinquency.html

8: Social Diffusion

122. Cohen-Cole, E., and Fletcher, J. M. (2008). 'Detecting implausible social network effects in acne, height, and headaches: longitudinal analysis', *BMJ*, *337*, a2533.

123. Fundraising in workplaces is a good way to test this kind of idea – the data are easy to access and understand, and the nudge we give the environment is sufficiently different from everyday practice to make the effects easy to see.

124. Organisation for Economic Cooperation and Development (OECD). (2018). 'Survey of Adult Skills (PIAAC)'. Retrieved from http://www.oecd.org/skills/piaac/

125. Also from the OECD Survey of Adult Skills.

126. Gershon, R., Cryder, C., and John, L. K. (2018). 'The Reputational Benefits and Material Burdens of Prosocial Referral Incentives', *SSRN Electronic Journal.* http://dx.doi.org/10.2139/ssrn.3176019

9: Social Capital

127. Although the British monarchy is in many respects ceremonial, they enjoy a position at the centre of public life and play a role in representing Britain overseas.

128. The *Today* programme is a news and current affairs radio programme that has been running for 60 years on BBC Radio 4

(previously the BBC Home Service). Each year since 2003, between Christmas and New Year, the programme is guest edited by notable figures or celebrities.

129. Prince Harry was a soldier in the British army and served in Afghanistan in secret prior to being 'outed' by an Australian newspaper. He has been open about his own mental health struggles following his mother's death.

130. President Obama sends Invictus Games challenge to the Queen and Prince Harry – video. (2016, 29 April). *Guardian*. Retrieved from (https://www.theguardian.com/uk-news/video/2016/apr/29/president-obama-sends-invictus-games-challenge-to-the-queen-prince-harry-video

131. You might wonder why the families weren't just given money. We're not sure, but it's likely to be because money, unlike the vouchers, can be spent on anything and so might not have been used as intended; and because administering vouchers is a lot easier than administering cash payments, and harder to embezzle.

132. Because wealth is calculated as net assets minus net liabilities, someone with credit card debt and no savings can easily have negative wealth.

10: Social Support

133. Education Endowment Foundation. (2018). Magic Breakfast. Retrieved from https://educationendowmentfoundation.org.uk/projects-and-evaluation/projects/magic-breakfast/

134. Education Endowment Foundation. (2018). Philosophy for children. Retrieved from https://educationendowmentfoundation.org.uk/projects-and-evaluation/projects/philosophy-for-children/

135. Education Endowment Foundation. (2018). Visible Classroom. Retrieved from https://educationendowmentfoundation.org.uk/projects-and-evaluation/projects/the-visible-classroom/

136. Education Endowment Foundation. (2018). Teaching assistants. Retrieved from https://educationendowmentfoundation.org.uk/evidence-summaries/teaching-learning-toolkit/teaching-assistants/

137. https://educationendowmentfoundation.org.uk/projects-and-evaluation/projects/texting-parents/

138. Linos, E., Sanders, M., & Ní Chonaire, A. (2019). It's nice to be nice, but it's good to be smart. *Forthcoming.*
139. Diabetes UK (2016). Facts and stats. Retrieved from https://diabetes-resources-production.s3-eu-west-1.amazonaws.com/diabetes-storage/migration/pdf/DiabetesUK_Facts_Stats_Oct16.pdf
140. The State of Obesity (2018). Diabetes in the United States. Retrieved from https://stateofobesity.org/diabetes/
141. World Health Organization (WHO) (2017). Diabetes Factsheet. Retrieved from http://www.who.int/mediacentre/factsheets/fs312/en/
142. Middle-aged men twice as likely to have diabetes as women. (2009, 13 July). Diabetes UK. Retrieved from https://www.diabetes.org.uk/about_us/news_landing_page/middle-aged-men-twice-as-likely-to-have-diabetes-as-women

11: Social Bridging

143. People were kept on the platform for safeguarding reasons, and the platform was monitored 24/7 – so if someone said something that was detected as inappropriate, or reported abuse, someone from the safeguarding team was alerted and took appropriate action.
144. Milkround (2018). 'The Times top 100 graduate employers 2017–18'. Retrieved from https://advice.milkround.com/the-times-top-100-graduate-employers

12: Role Models

145. Social mobility in this case is defined as someone who is born into the bottom 20 per cent of households by income moving to the top 20 per cent by middle age.
146. In fact, all education prior to getting a PhD increases your expected earnings over your lifetime. Because of the time it takes, and the fact that it limits your career options afterwards, a PhD is a bad financial investment.
147. Eton College website – destination data, analysis of last ten years (2006–2015), authors' own analysis.
148. Wells, in the north of the county, is technically a city by virtue of having a cathedral, but with a population of 10,000 in the 2011

census it is much smaller than Somerset's county town of Taunton (Source: UK 2011 census data).

149. Although the Russell Group is ultimately a fee-paying membership organization, it consists largely of the most selective institutions in the country, including Oxford and Cambridge universities, and is widely used by the public and the press as a proxy for high-quality universities.

150. Department for Education (2017). Statistics on Destinations from Key Stage 5 by local authority. Retrieved from https://www.gov.uk/government/statistics/destinations-of-ks4-and-ks5-pupils-2016 - authors' own analysis.

151. The Somerset Challenge (2014). *What is the Somerset Challenge?* Retrieved from https://slp.somerset.org.uk/sites/sa/challenge/SitePages/Home.aspx

152. Soman, D. (2015). *The last mile: Creating social and economic value from behavioural insights.* Toronto, Canada: University of Toronto Press.

153. Over the course of their lives, they will end up paying more money, and probably for longer. However, the return on the loans to the British government is estimated to be slightly less than 50 pence in the pound – that is, most of the loans will never be repaid.

154. Osborne actually went to St Paul's, a different elite private school, but in the popular perception gives off a very Etonian vibe.

155. This research study was written up as Silva, A. S., Ni Chonaire, A., & Sanders, M. (2016). Does the heart rule the head? Economic and emotional incentives for university attendance. London, UK: the Behavioural Insights Team.

156. Hoxby, C., & Turner, S. (2013). Expanding college opportunities for high-achieving, low-income students. *Stanford Institute for Economic Policy Research Discussion Paper*, (12–014).

157. School performance here is based on one of two measures – either the Department for Education's Progress 8 measure or ratings awarded by the Office for Standards in Education (Ofsted), the inspectorate for schools in England.

158. Based on the 2011 census data.

159. The Progress 8 ratings, although designed to reduce the extent to which school-performance measures are just a reflection of social

class, are almost perfectly predicted by the socio-economic status of the school's students.

160. Dasgupta, N. (2011). Ingroup Experts and Peers as Social Vaccines Who Inoculate the Self-Concept: The Stereotype Inoculation Model. *Psychological Inquiry, 22*(4), 231–46.

161. Sanders, M., Reinstein, D., & Tupper, A. (2014). *Worth 1000 Words: The Effect of Social Cues on a Fundraising Campaign in a Government Agency: a Field Experiment.* Bristol, UK: Centre for Market and Public Organisation.

13: Belonging and Trusting

162. Change.Org. (2018). Bring Priya and her beautiful family back home to Biloela, Queensland. Retrieved from https://www.change.org/p/peter-dutton-bring-priya-back-to-biloela

163. Annett, T. (2018, May 2). Biloela asylum seeker mum 'in tears'. *The Observer.* Retrieved from https://www.gladstoneobserver.com.au/news/biloela-asylum-seeker-mum-tears-ahead-life-changin/3404591/

164. Leary, M. R., & Baumeister, R. F. (2017). The need to belong: Desire for interpersonal attachments as a fundamental human motivation. In *Interpersonal Development* (pp. 57–89). London, UK: Routledge.

165. Hornsey, M. J., & Jetten, J. (2004). The individual within the group: Balancing the need to belong with the need to be different. *Personality and Social Psychology Review, 8*(3), 248–64.

166. Leary, M. R., & Baumeister, R. F. (2017). The need to belong: Desire for interpersonal attachments as a fundamental human motivation. In *Interpersonal Development* (pp. 57–89). London, UK: Routledge.

167. Kitchen, P., Williams, A., & Chowhan, J. (2012). Sense of community belonging and health in Canada: A regional analysis. *Social Indicators Research, 107*(1), 103–26.

168. Bond, L., Butler, H., Thomas, L., Carlin, J., Glover, S., Bowes, G., & Patton, G. (2007). Social and school connectedness in early secondary school as predictors of late teenage substance use, mental health, and academic outcomes. *Journal of Adolescent Health, 40*(4), 357–e9.

169. Luo, Y., Hawkley, L. C., Waite, L. J., & Cacioppo, J. T. (2012).

Loneliness, health, and mortality in old age: A national longitudinal study. *Social Science & Medicine*, 74(6), 907–14.

170. Tellhed, U., Bäckström, M., & Björklund, F. (2017). Will I fit in and do well? The importance of social belongingness and self-efficacy for explaining gender differences in interest in STEM and HEED majors. *Sex Roles*, 77(1–2), 86–96.

171. Glass, C. R., & Westmont, C. M. (2014). Comparative effects of belongingness on the academic success and cross-cultural interactions of domestic and international students. *International Journal of Intercultural Relations*, 38, 106–19.

172. Cohen, G. L., & Garcia, J. (2008). Identity, belonging, and achievement: A model, interventions, implications. *Current Directions in Psychological Science*, 17(6), 365–9.

173. O'Reilly, J., & Robinson, S. L. (2009). The negative impact of ostracism on thwarted belongingness and workplace contributions. In *Academy of management proceedings* (Vol. 2009, No. 1, pp. 1–7). Briarcliff Manor, NY: Academy of Management.

174. Armstrong, D., Shakespeare-Finch, J., & Shochet, I. (2016). Organizational belongingness mediates the relationship between sources of stress and posttrauma outcomes in firefighters. *Psychological Trauma: Theory, Research, Practice, and Policy*, 8(3), 343.

175. Verhagen, M., Lodder, G. M., & Baumeister, R. F. (2018). Unmet belongingness needs but not high belongingness needs alone predict adverse well-being: A response surface modeling approach. *Journal of Personality*, 86(3), 498–507.

176. Pickett, C. L., Gardner, W. L., & Knowles, M. (2004). Getting a cue: The need to belong and enhanced sensitivity to social cues. *Personality and Social Psychology Bulletin*, 30(9), 1095–107.

177. Cohen, G. L., & Garcia, J. (2008). Identity, belonging, and achievement: A model, interventions, implications. *Current Directions in Psychological Science*, 17(6), 365–9.

178. Dearden, L. (2017, August 24). 'I don't feel welcome anymore': EU citizens explain why they are leaving the UK in their thousands, *Independent*. Retrieved from https://www.independent.co.uk/news/uk/home-news/eu-migration-uk-brexit-referendum-latest-net-fall-figures-why-racism-hate-crime-brexodus-government-a7911196.html

179. Sime, D. (2018). Here to Stay? Project. Retrieved from http://www.migrantyouth.org/

180. Porta, R. L., Lopez-De-Silane, F., Schleifer, A., & Vishny, R. W. (1996). *Trust in large organizations* (No. w5864). National Bureau of Economic Research.
181. According to the Harry Potter wiki (http://harrypotter.wikia.com/wiki/House_Cup), the Slytherin v Gryffindor dyad have won the House cup every year for which records are available since 1985, noting that the cup was suspended during the Second Wizarding War.
182. The way that unemployment benefits are withdrawn as beneficiaries find paid employment means that many low-income individuals face an effective tax rate of more than 80 per cent –which limits the incentive to work more.

Acknowledgements

It's taken us just over a year to write this book, pulling together research from academia, from our colleagues at the Behavioural Insights Team – as well as our own – and examples from across government. It's not the book that we set out to write originally, and has to a great extent been shaped by the events of the last few years and the increasingly bleak regard in which social influence, and particularly social media networks, are held.

This journey would not have been possible without our friends and colleagues at the Behavioural Insights Team, the Social Mobility and Student Success Division, and the Policy Institute at King's College London. At BIT in particular, we have seen first-hand a different way of viewing the world – one that is more realistic in its account of human behaviour than standard economics, and more creative in its application of that knowledge than the approach governments have traditionally taken. Many of the ideas we recount in this book are based on trials conducted by BIT: a reflection both of our adoption of that viewpoint, and of BIT's status as the world leader in this area.

We want to offer special thanks to a few colleagues in particular, especially to David Halpern, BIT's CEO, who has been a mentor and inspiration to us over our time at BIT, and who first encouraged us to write this book.

Special thanks should also go to Clare Delargy, Bibi Groot and Eliza Kozman, whose work on social bridging, social support and role models gives us hope for the future and was fundamental to the latter half of the book; to Michael Hallsworth, whose work on social norms was in many ways the trial that launched a thousand ships; and to Charlotte Bearn, the former head of BI Ventures, who facilitated the construction of two products – Promptable and Networky – which helped make these ideas a reality.

Much of the work we've written about in this book could not have happened without the enthusiastic collaboration and support of our partners. We'd like to particularly thank Anne-Marie Canning from King's College London, Michael Lynas and Naim Moukarzel at the National Citizen Service, and the wonderful staff at all the schools and further education colleges, businesses and governments who took the time out of their already busy and demanding jobs to collaborate with us.

We're also grateful to Kate Glazebrook, Ryan Buell, Alison Wood-Brooks, Katy Milkman, Michael Lynas, Mike Luca, Dave Rand and countless others, whose conversations through the years have informed our thinking. Michael would especially like to thank Max Bazerman and Michael Norton for their contribution to his personal social capital, welcoming him with open arms into a world he would never otherwise have known and making him feel like he belonged there.

We're also grateful to Annabel Price, who helped us to pull together many of the essential but less sexy parts of the book, and without whom we would have enjoyed this process less, and to Jo Stansall, our editor at Michael O'Mara Books, who commissioned this book and has helped shape our thoughts into the manuscript you've just read.

Picture Credits

Page 27: 'Deplorables and proud'; TwinsofSedona / WikiMedia / public domain

Page 33: *The traitor: degradation of Alfred Drefus* (1895); Henri Meyer / Bibliothèque nationale de France / Wikimedia / public domain

Page 47: Second World War propaganda poster: *Our Carelessness, Their Secret Weapon, Prevent Forest Fires*; US National Archives and Records Administration

Page 52: Rumour cascade image; from 'Rumour cascades', https://www.aaai.org/ocs/index.php/ICWSM/ICWSM14/paper/viewFile/8122/8110

Page 63: A rendering from Facebook to show how one of its new ads would look; Facebook

Page 86: Stick figures in diagram; Shutterstock

Page 97: Google team picture; Keng Susumpov (kengz) / Flickr / CC BY 2.0

Page 149: BIT lunch photo; author's own

Page 187: Photo of Pete and Jamie's wedding ceremony; author's own

Index